The Complete Tarot: Learn The Tarot For Beginners & Advanced

© **Copyright 2019 by Sofia Visconti - All rights reserved.**

This document is geared towards providing exact and reliable information in regards to the topic and issue covered. The publication is sold with the idea that the publisher is not required to render accounting, officially permitted or otherwise qualified services. If advice is necessary, legal or professional, a practiced individual in the profession should be ordered.

From a Declaration of Principles which was accepted and approved equally by a Committee of the American Bar Association and a Committee of Publishers and Associations.

In no way is it legal to reproduce, duplicate, or transmit any part of this document in either electronic means or in printed format. Recording of this publication is strictly prohibited, and any storage of this document is not allowed unless with written permission from the publisher. All rights reserved.

The information provided herein is stated to be truthful and consistent, in that any liability, in terms of inattention or otherwise, by any usage or abuse of any policies, processes, or directions contained within is the solitary and utter responsibility of the recipient reader. Under no circumstances will any legal responsibility or blame be held against the publisher for any reparation, damages, or monetary loss due to the information herein, either directly or indirectly.

Respective authors own all copyrights not held by the publisher.

The information herein is offered for informational purposes solely and is universal as so. The presentation of the information is without a contract or any type of guarantee assurance.

The trademarks that are used are without any consent, and the publication of the trademark is without permission or backing by the trademark owner. All trademarks and brands within this book are for clarifying purposes only and are owned by the owners themselves, not affiliated with this document.

Tarot for Beginners: Begin Your Exploration & Reveal The Mysteries & Wonder of The Tarot, Tarot Card Meanings, Spreads, Numerology & More

Table Of Contents

Table Of Contents

Introduction

Chapter 1. Tarot 101: An Overview
    A Brief History of the Tarot Cards
    Rider-Waite Tarot Cards
    Kabbalah and Astrology
    The Major and Minor Arcana of the Tarot Cards

Chapter 2. How to Prepare Yourself for Tarot Reading
    Attuning Your Energy With a New Tarot Deck
    Cleansing Your Tarot Cards Before Reading
    How to Protect Your Tarot Cards
    Preparing the Space for Tarot Reading
    How to Choose Tarot Cards for Reading
    How to Turn Over the Cards
    Tarot Card Interpretations
    How to Start Reading the Tarot Cards
    Read the Numbers in the Cards
    Read the Card Elements
    Read the Card Colors
    Avoid Reversed Card Interpretations

Chapter 3. Tarot Card Layouts
    Daily Tarot Card
    Three Card Reading
    Yes or No Reading
    The Celtic Cross
    The Weekly Forecast
    The Tree of Life Layout
    The Chakra Spread

Chapter 4. Interpreting the Major Arcana Cards
- The Fool
- The Magician
- The High Priestess
- The Empress
- The Emperor
- The Hierophant
- The Lovers
- The Chariot
- Strength
- The Hermit
- The Wheel of Fortune
- Justice
- The Hanged Man
- Death
- Temperance
- The Devil
- The Tower
- The Star
- The Moon
- The Sun
- Judgement
- The World

Chapter 5. Interpreting Minor Arcana Cards: The Suit Of Wands
- The King of Wands
- The Queen of Wands
- The Knight of Wands
- The Page of Wands
- Ten of Wands
- Nine of Wands
- Eight of Wands

Seven of Wands
Six of Wands
Five of Wands
Four of Wands
Three of Wands
Two of Wands
Ace of Wands

Chapter 6. Interpreting Minor Arcana Cards: The Suit Of Swords

King of Swords
Queen of Swords
Knight of Swords
Page of Swords
Ten of Swords
Nine of Swords
Eight of Swords
Seven of Swords
Six of Swords
Five of Swords
Four of Swords
Three of Swords
Two of Swords
Ace of Swords
Character: Ace of Swords

Chapter 7. Interpreting Minor Arcana Cards: The Suit Of Pentacles

King of Pentacles
Queen of Pentacles
Knight of Pentacles
Page of Pentacles
Ten of Pentacles

Nine of Pentacles
Eight of Pentacles
Seven of Pentacles
Six of Pentacles
Five of Pentacles
Four of Pentacles
Three of Pentacles
Two of Pentacles
Ace of Pentacles

Chapter 8. Interpreting Minor Arcana Cards: The Suit Of Cups
King of Cups
Queen of Cups
Knight of Cups
Page of Cups
The Ten of Cups
The Upright Ten of Cups
Nine of Cups
The Upright Nine of Cups
Eight of Cups
Seven of Cups
The Reversed Seven of Cups
Six of Cups
Five of Cups
Four of Cups
Three of Cups
Two of Cups
Ace of Cups

Conclusion

Introduction

This beginner's guide book will help you learn everything you need to know about Tarot cards - its history, principles, philosophy, and how you can use the deck for daily practical affirmation and long-term spiritual development.

Contrary to popular belief, you don't need psychic ability before you can read the Tarot. You can greatly benefit from the Tarot's insights so long as you have an open mind and you are willing to trust the impressions you feel during a reading.

Benefits of Learning Tarot Card Reading

There is no hocus pocus involved, when you learn how to read tarot cards, you will be able to become attuned to your own self and therefore connect with your intuition.

Tarot reading will allow you to become much more aware of yourself and your surroundings. The increased perceptiveness can benefit you in multiple ways; it can help you improve your relationships with your loved ones, and it can help you pinpoint the areas of your lives that could use a bit more attention, if not improvement.

A tarot reading also has a surprising benefit; it can help you in making difficult decisions. Keep in mind that tarot cards cannot really predict your future or tell you in detail about what exactly you need to do. What they can do is help you find what you want.

Another little known benefit is that it can help you find peace. Some people tend to obsess over what could go wrong. A tarot reading can help you see the positive side of things and find calmness.

How This Book Will Help You

We will start with the fundamentals - the deck's structure, its relation to astrology, Kabbala, and numerology. Then we will explore the different layouts used by Tarot readers today.

You may try conventional spreads, but take note that there's no right or wrong way to read a card. Some people pick one card every day and that's it, while some people spread as much as 20 cards in one reading.

To start with, you may want to read the keywords for the card interpretations at the start of Chapter 4, 5, 6, 7, and 8.

In the detailed interpretations, you will learn the card's alternative names, astrological associations, and numbers that will provide you additional insight.

While there are different versions of the Tarot deck, and different readers have their different interpretations due to the development of this craft for centuries, this book aims to provide you a foundation from which to start.

The Tarot cards capture the mind and the soul of the human experience. Each card reflects your state of mind and stage of life. Over the centuries, people have used the Tarot for predicting the future, enhancing their knowledge of the mystical worlds, gain spiritual insight, and receive instruction from the divine.

The esoteric symbols that you will encounter in the Tarot cards are intended to stimulate our intuition and connect us with our inner divinity. Regular reading of the Tarot cards can provide you a lot of benefits such as:

- Improved self-awareness - The Tarot cards can provide you the time and space to concentrate on yourself.

- Increased creativity - Tarot reading can provide a different angle on your situation and creative ways to resolve conflict.

- Situational awareness that may manifest in intuitiveness - The Tarot cards can help you to have a glimpse of the immediate future and how they are influenced by the people around you.

- The ability to help others - Through the insights from the cards, you can improve your ability to empower others to discover their spiritual journey.

- Enhanced Spirituality - Tarot reading allows you to see the world and connect to it on a whole new level

Once you become adept in Tarot reading, hopefully you will remember something in this book that will spark your imagination and contribute to this rich mystical art.

Regardless of your purpose in learning the Tarot cards, I encourage you to share with me the journey of this esoteric wisdom and partake from the greater insights into yourself and the people you care for.

Chapter 1. Tarot 101: An Overview

The Tarot is an archetypal map of human consciousness that goes beyond our journey through life both in practical and spiritual.

Reading the Tarot cards is the practice of divination through a particular layout or spread of cards.

But contrary to common belief, Tarot reading is not all about fortune telling, and you don't need to possess psychic powers before you can read the cards.

The Tarot cards are used to provide insight into the deepest trust of our higher consciousness. They provide an evolved awareness of what we already know deep within.

A Brief History of the Tarot Cards

Conventional playing cards were first noted in Europe in the 14th century. These cards were believed to have been originated in the Middle East where they had been part of the society as amusement for many centuries.

However, Tarot expert Tadfor Little claims that these were not Tarot cards, saying that there's no conclusive proof that the modern day Tarot cards or anything resembling them have been created at that time.

The origin of the Tarot cards, or at least the precursor of what would be the modern Tarot deck can be traced back to the mid-15th century in a letter written by the Duke of Milan asking for a few decks of "triumph" cards that will be used for a special occasion. In this letter, it was made apparent these cards were not at all like regular playing cards.

However, it was also established that these early cards were meant to be used for entertainment and not for divination. People used the decks to play a card game called triumph, which has some semblance to bridge. The game immediately became popular across Europe, and people started to call them as *tarocchi* or the Italian word for Tarot around the 16th century.

The deck was called the Visconti-Sforza cards because they were commissioned by Francesco Visconti - the Duke of Milan.

Even though the Catholic Church called the triumph cards as the devil's picture book (probably because they were used for gambling) these cards have predominantly Christian imagery and themes.

The card sequence recounts a story about a young man who died and was reborn as the Fool. This is the reason why this particular sequence (known as Major Arcana) is often called the Journey of the Fool.

The deck also depicts angels, a male and female Pope, the Devil, and the four virtues. Other characters were the magician, the knight, the queen, the king, lovers, old man, the innocent youth, the father, the mother, and the wise woman.

Some sources reveal that the knowledge of the Tarot might have preceded even the Visconti-Sforza cards.

In the 1300s, Johannes von Rheinfelden (a German Monk) wrote about a series of painted cards, which worked as a symbolic depiction of the journey of life and soul.

Some historians also believe that Gnostic groups might have used some form of Tarot cards to teach illiterate people about the interplay of opposites or dualism. Hence, there is the possibility that the cards might have been used to express and also teach Christian knowledge.

In the 1800s, occult followers in Europe discovered Tarot cards. They believed that the images in the cards have more meaning than mere entertainment. They began using the cards as a tool for divination, and occult masters wrote extensively about it. As such, the tarot became part of the occult practices.

However, there are historians who believe that these cards have Egyptian origins. The cards are believed to be derived from the only surviving book from the ancient library of Alexandria and hold the keys to the mysteries of life. (More on this a bit later).

Tarot reading has survived the test of time and has gained popularity in the modern world. More recently, Tarot designs can be seen in the fashion collections presented by major fashion houses like Versace.

It is also interesting to note that there are now online Tarot readers that are using internet technology and social media to provide readings to millions of people around the world.

Rider-Waite Tarot Cards

Different styles and versions of Tarot cards have been created through the years. In this book, we will use the Universal Waite, which is an improved Rider-Waite cards.

The classic Rider-Waite deck was developed by A.E. Waite, who is one of the founding members of the Golden Dawn Order. Waite published the deck in 1909 in London.

This is regarded as the most popular Tarot deck and has inspired numerous variations and styles.

Some Tarot enthusiasts call this deck as the Rider-Waite Smith as a way to honor Pamela C. Smith who was another member of the Golden Dawn Order and illustrated the deck.

Under the direction of Waite, Smith used the Sola Busca artwork to draw the images in the Tarot. This is the reason why there are numerous resemblances in the symbolism between the final Rider-Waite and Sola Busca. The latter is an earlier version of the Tarot cards.

Smith was noted as the first artist to use characters to represent images in the lower cards. Rather than drawing a group of swords, wands, coins, or cups, Smith added human figures in the decks.

The imagery of the Rider-Waite is heavily inspired by Kabbalistic traditions. As a result, an overview about the Kabbalah is often included in Tarot instructional books.

Today, more than a hundred years since the publication of the Rider-Waite Smith deck, Tarot decks are available in endless options of designs.

Basically, many of these are still inspired by the Rider-Waite Smith, even though each card has its own distinct style.

Kabbalah and Astrology

The term 'occult' may have negative associations. However, it really means hidden knowledge. The dark connotation linked with the Tarot started in 1781 when the Antoine Court de Gebelin, a French Freemason, published his treatise entitled Monde Primitif.

In this treatise, Gebelin claimed that the Tarot cards were in fact the pages from the Book of Thoth or the Ancient Egyptian Book of Wisdom. Thoth is the Egyptian god of wisdom, healing, and also the occult.

The beliefs propagated by Gebelin's treatise emerged as part of the revival of the occult in the late 19th century when ancient wisdom was used by Napoleon when he invaded Egypt and the West started its awareness and eventual fascination of Egyptian artifacts.

The early works of De Gebelin was continued by Jean-Baptiste Alliette, another member of the French Freemason and was popularly known as Etteilla.

Alliette developed the possible links of the Tarot to the Kabbalah, which is the arcane belief system based in the early Judaism.

Later on, another Frenchman, Eliphas Levi, further promoted Tarot as part of the occult. Levi popularized the link of the 22 cards of the major arcana to the 22 letters of the Hebrew alphabet. He claims that this corresponds to the pathways depicted in the Tree of Life.

A.E. White, the creator of the Rider-Waite cards, was influenced by the works of Levi.

White, together with his colleagues at the Golden Dawn Order, integrated astrological, Kabbalah, and Egyptian mysticism to develop the Tarot associations, which have become accepted today by Tarot enthusiasts.

Even though Tarot has collected numerous associations with the occult over the years, these mystical cards basically reflect the beliefs of their creators.

The survivability and adaptability of the Tarot cards resulted in different decks, from Steampunk to Wiccan, vampires, to Angels, and Fairies to Modern.

Even though these decks are presented in contemporary decks, the cards ultimately connect to us through its symbolism and our infinite reflection.

The Major and Minor Arcana of the Tarot Cards

The standard Tarot deck consists of 78 cards, and is further divided into two categories: 22 major arcana cards and 56 minor arcana cards.

The term arcana is derived from the word arcane, which means esoteric or secret.

The cards of the Major Arcana signify important life events or changes, while the cards of the Minor Arcana reflect our everyday struggles.

The Minor Arcana cards are seen as being more comprehensive aspects of the Major Arcana cards.

The Cards of the Major Arcana

The 22 Major Arcana cards can be referred to collectively as trumps or keys and singularly as arcanum. These cards are numbered from 0 (the Fool) to XX1 (The World).

While there's no definitive proof on the provenance of the Major Arcana cards, some believe that the word trump originated from a game called Triumphs.

Triumphs was derived from the classic card game Trionfi, which was popular in France in Italy.

In this card game, trump cards that correspond to the characters in the Major Arcana outrank other cards.

For instance, the High Priestess outranks the Magician, while the Magician outranks the Fool.

Meanwhile, researcher Gertrude Moakley also suggested the Milanese carnival origin of the Major Arcana cards.

The said carnival has its origins to Saturnalia, which is believed to be the pagan origin of Christmas celebration.

During Saturnalia, Milanese dressed as Tarot characters and paraded in carriages throughout the city.

The Saturnalia origin could be plausible because it was the Duke of Milan who was noted to have commissioned the first Tarot cards.

The Cards of the Minor Arcana

The remaining 56 cards are collectively known as the Minor Arcana, and they are grouped into four suits: Cups, Swords, Wands, and Pentacles.

Each suit consists of 14 cards from Ace to 10 then court cards - the King, Queen, Knight, and Page.

The four suits of each card have a ruling element, and each corresponds to certain aspects of life:

Suit	Element	Life Area
Wands	Fire	Communication, Travel, Instinct
Swords	Air	Decisions, Intellect
Pentacles	Earth	Achievement, Money, Property
Cups	Water	Relationships, Emotions

Meanwhile, popular psychologist Carl Jung summarized the mental processes of the human mind into four primary functions, which could be associated with each suit of the Minor Arcana.

Suit	Element	Mind Functions
Wands	Fire	I desire
Swords	Air	I think
Pentacles	Earth	I possess
Cups	Water	I feel

The court cards of the Minor Arcana are also associated with certain elements:

Character	Element
Knights	Fire
Queens	Water
Knights	Air

Pages	Earth

So for instance, the Queen of Pentacles is Water of the Suit of Earth, while the Knight of Swords is Fire of the Suit of Air.

Learning the essential concepts of the elements will provide meaning for your cards. So for example, the Knight of Cups, combining Air and Water suggests a connection between your decisions or intellect with relationships or emotions.

Chapter 2. How to Prepare Yourself for Tarot Reading

Like people, Tarot cards are influenced by energy. The cards can absorb your energy during readings. Even the energy of those who touch the cards can be affected.

This is why it is crucial not to allow other people to touch your cards without any purpose. Your Tarot cards embody your energies as well as your intentions. Your cards are personal to you.

So before we dig in deeper, you need to perform specific rituals so you can align your energy with your new deck, cleanse the cards before reading, and cast a shield to them prior to safekeeping.

Attuning Your Energy With a New Tarot Deck

Attuning refers to the process of connecting your energy with a new set of Tarot cards. The stronger your connection with your cards, the more inspiring, insightful, and accurate your readings could be.

Before you start reading a new deck of Tarot cards, it is important to attune them by placing the cards under your pillow for seven days.

You should also be familiar with the cards by touching them and looking at them every day. This will allow your energy to be imprinted in the deck.

Also, you can try visualization to further attune your energy with the cards.

Follow these steps for attuning your Tarot cards:

1. Use your right hand to hold the new cards. It is important to use the right hand because this is called the giving hand. In this way, you are giving your cards your personal energy.

2. Take a deep breath, close your eyes, and try to visualize a pure light coming down from your forehead, going through your neck, then heart, then down to your arm, and into your right hand, and going into your new deck.

3. See your cards being filled with pure light.

4. If you are aware of your angel or spirit guides, ask for their assistance. Specifically ask for their protection.

5. Slowly open your eyes when you feel that you are ready.

Cleansing Your Tarot Cards Before Reading

Always remember to dispel any stagnant energy whenever you take out your Tarot cards. You can do this through the following steps:

1. Use your right hand to hold your cards and blow air on them.

2. Just gently blow on the edges of the card. Just one breath is enough.

3. Place the cards in a neat pile but don't let them go.

4. Firmly knock on the top of the cards once. After this, your card is already cleansed of stagnant energy, and you can use it for reading.

How to Protect Your Tarot Cards

Once you have performed the attunement, your Tarot cards already contain your energy imprint.

Similar to people, Tarot cards are also capable of picking up negative or excessive energy from people and even places. These uninvited energies could affect your readings.

So, it is important that you protect your cards when you are not using them.

Basically you need to wrap the cards using a dark-colored cloth. Silk or cotton are recommended. Also use a box or bag in storing them, and store them alone (Don't mix them up with mundane things).

For extra protection, you can keep the cards with certain crystals, such as amethyst or clear quartz.

Preparing the Space for Tarot Reading

The space where you perform the Tarot reading should be filled with positive vibes. This space should be peaceful, and must provide you comfort and relaxation.

Be sure that your reading space has a clean, flat surface where you can place your cards on.

Some Tarot readers place a reading cloth to protect the cards from physical or energy harm.

The reading cloth is often the cloth you use to wrap your cards when you keep them. However, any kind of fabric will do as long as it is clean.

You may choose to perform a simple ritual before you start the reading. This ritual is done to honor this practice.

Remember, our thoughts can create reality and helps in manifesting a strong connection between the Tarot cards, ourselves, and the person for whom you are performing the reading.

Tarot reading will also involve your spirit guides, if you are already aware of them.

Below is the suggested ritual to help you get started. However, you can personalize your own preparation as you enhance your reading skills.

1. Light a candle (preferably a white one) and put it near your reading space.

2. Take three to five deep breaths and close your eyes.

3. As described in the attunement ritual, visualize a pure light flowing from your head and into your cards.

4. You may also choose to set the intention to enjoy the best Tarot reading you want to experience

5. After you complete your reading, you can affirm your mind that the reading is over.

6. Express gratitude for the insights you have received and keep your Tarot cards in a safe place.

7. Don't forget to blow out the candle.

How to Choose Tarot Cards for Reading

First, you need to learn how to shuffle the deck. Remember to always be relaxed so your energy will not be disturbed. Also clarify your intentions.

To select the cards for a reading, you may either cut the deck or use the fan method.

Cutting the deck is ideal for specific layouts that require a lot of cards like the Tree of Life or Celtic Cross. On the other hand, the fan method is best if you just need a few cards for the reading.

Cutting the Tarot Deck

If you are reading the cards for yourself, cut the deck two times using your left hand.

The left hand is used as this is the hand of fate.

You should have three piles for this method. Select one pile to place on top of the deck and place the other two piles under your chosen pile.

Choose a layout (you will learn the different layouts later). Deal the cards from the top of the deck and place them face down in your front.

If you are reading for another person, you should ask the recipient to perform the steps mentioned above except for the layout.

Fan Method

If you are reading for yourself, spread the Tarot cards face down to resemble a fan. Randomly select the cards from the fan using your left hand. The cards should be placed facedown and must follow the spread layout that you have chosen.

If you are reading for another person, ask him or her to shuffle the cards. Take the cards and place the cards to resemble a fan. Let the recipient randomly select the cards from the fan using the left hand.

Get the cards he or she selected then place them using the layout you have chosen. Remember to keep the cards facedown.

How to Turn Over the Cards

You should also follow a specific method in turning over the cards.

Whenever you are turning over the Tarot cards, avoid flipping them from top to bottom or the other way around. Instead, you should flip them over from left to right.

The wrong way of flipping the cards could turn the cards upside down, which will provide you a different insight.

Later in this chapter, we will discuss the meaning of cards in reverse.

Tarot Card Interpretations

Each card of the Tarot deck offers a lot of symbolism and potential meanings. Before looking up the meaning of each card, try to consider them first by thinking about what specific aspect of the card you are attracted to fits.

Your inner divinity can usually direct you to the most suitable meaning of the card for interpretation.

The cards may even provide different relevance every time you encounter them.

If you are reading the cards for other people, your intuition will guide you to read the cards differently.

There will be instances that you will start a reading and you can't make a sense of what the cards are trying to tell you. In this case, you need to shuffle the cards again and use another layout. If the same cards come up again, then you should proceed with the reading.

Always relax and tune in to the images depicted in the cards. The traditional meanings of each card are only a guide, and your intuition should prevail.

Do you have the Ten of Wands in your chosen cards? Then it might mean that it is not the right time to read the cards because there's too much going on in your life now. It is best to wait for several days before you try again. When you are reading for another person, the feeling of being blocked may be reflected by the state of mind of the recipient.

If your mind is blank, ask the recipient to allow her feelings and intentions to surface. Doubt can also affect the quality of energy needed to provide meaningful interpretation.

How to Start Reading the Tarot Cards

Reading the Tarot cards is both pleasurable and enlightening. It is a skill that you cannot master in one sitting. It requires time, practice, and intuition to learn how to do it.

Tarot experts suggest the following tips to start your journey.

Listen to Your Intuition

Many beginners in Tarot card reading are guided to be drawn to specific symbols on each card. Every card in the Tarot deck is filled with symbols. However, you will realize that you are only drawn to one or two features.

Your intuition guides you to these symbols, and you need to improve this aspect so you can be better in card reading. Don't concern yourself too much about the meanings of each card described in this book. Just allow your intuition to guide you and tell the story.

To improve your skills in reading, try to refer to the summary interpretations that you will find in Chapter 4 and Chapter 5, then go back to the images for each card. Focusing on the image as long as you can boost your intuition that is important to a reading, while reading the words could engage the left part of your brain or the logical area.

Your left brain will trigger your inner judge and will bug you with questions if you are reading the cards right. Remember, your interpretation of the cards prevail over the traditional meaning of the cards.

You can learn the comprehensive card interpretations when you are not reading the cards so you can improve your knowledge. But to start with, look at the pictures first. This will help you ready any kind of deck and not just the Rider-Waite Smith deck.

Start with the Major Arcana

If you are just learning, you can start with the cards of the Major Arcana. You can progress with the full 78 cards if you are more confident in your skill.

The cards in the Major Arcana denotes the primary energies, while the cards in the Minor Arcana refines these primary energies. Because the Minor Arcana cards support the Major

Arcana, you will not miss out any significant information by starting with the major cards at this stage.

The Major Arcana cards will provide you a reading for significant interpretations.

Read the Numbers in the Cards

The Tarot cards are also influenced by numerology, which is the esoteric art of interpreting mystical numbers.

The numbers in the Tarot deck have the following meanings that also correspond to the suit in the cards:

NUMBER	MEANING
1	New beginning, new energies
2	Balance, partnerships, division
3	Acknowledgement
4	Boundaries, stability
5	Challenges, instability

6	Improvement, harmony
7	Ambitions, potential
8	Progress, rewards
9	Intensity
10	Endings, completion

Every suit in the Tarot deck modifies the meaning of the numbers. So the Three of Cups could mean celebration, while the Three of Swords may mean betrayal or sorrow. You can devise your own interpretations by combining the meaning of the suit and the numbers.

Read the Card Elements

Another easy way to read the cards is to focus on the elements of each suit.

For instance, the Earth element in the suit of Pentacles signifies planning, structure or finances, while the Fire element in the suit of Wands signifies action and creativity.

The element of Water in the suit of Cups signifies relationships and emotions, while the element of Air in the suit of Swords calls for the need to make decisions and mental clarity.

Read the Card Colors

While reading the cards, you may find yourself attracted to one or more colors shown in the card. Refer to the following guide to interpret their meanings:

COLOR	MEANING
Yellow	Self-expression, illumination, consciousness
Gray	Unknown outcomes
White	Innocence, purity
Red	Passion, energy
Green	Growth, nature
Blue	Clarity, truth
Black	Oppression, protection

Purple	Spirituality, intuition
Orange	Creativity, impulse

Avoid Reversed Card Interpretations

If you are just learning the Tarot cards, it is best to stay away from the meanings of the reverse cards.

What if you get a reversed card? Just turn them up immediately and concentrate on your responses to the card in its upright position.

There are Tarot readers who are strictly adhering to the reversal interpretations, while other readers ignore them, even if they have already been practicing for years.

Just go with your own preference and follow your intuition.

But for knowledge sake, this book also includes the interpretations of reversed cards that you can learn in Chapter 4 and 5.

Chapter 3. Tarot Card Layouts

Over the years, countless card layouts have been developed by Tarot masters. However, the common layouts are the Week Ahead, 3-cards (Past, Present, and Future), the Celtic Cross.

You can try each layout and follow the one that you really like best.

Daily Tarot Card

Choosing one card every day is a great way to attune yourself with your Tarot.

Shuffle the deck, fan out or cut it, and select one card using your left hand.

Before revealing the card, ask yourself "What insight will help me today?"

Focus on the image of the card for interpretation or read the meaning of the cards in Chapter 4 and 5.

You may choose to display the card where you can see it regularly throughout the day, or you may also carry it with you.

Three Card Reading

The Three Card Reading method will help you remember your past, understand your present, and take a glimpse of your future. This is an easy way to use your Tarot cards.

Shuffle the deck, cut it or fan out, then lay three cards. If you want more insight, you may choose to add an extra card for every position, so you will have six cards.

You may also use this card reading method to look at the different aspects of your life such as Home, Money, Love, Spirit, Body, Mind.

You may also choose a Signifier card, which sums up the theme of a reading that you want to gain insight.

For instance, if you want to lay cards in one aspect such as Love, you can select a Signifier card from the deck instead of laying out a random card.

For a reading on love, you may take out the Lovers Card, and then shuffle the deck and choose your three cards.

Below is a list of Signifier cards and their corresponding life aspects:

CARD	ASPECT
Justice	Legal

Hierophant	Education
High Priestess	Psychic Development
Empress	Family and Fertility

Yes or No Reading

If you require an answer to a burning question, you can use the Yes-No reading:

1. Shuffle the deck then spread them face down in fan style.

2. Focus on asking the question in your mind.

3. Use your left hand to select one card and place it to your left.

4. Focus on the question again and select a second card. Place this card next to your first card.

5. Ask a question again and select another card. Place this card next to the second card.

6. Reveal the cards and refer to the list below to figure out if the answer is yes, no, or neutral.

The answer is affirmative if you get three yes cards.

The outcome is most likely positive if you get two yes cards and one no or neutral. However, the result may take some time to arrive.

Of course, the answer is negative if you get three no cards or a mix of no or neutral cards.

Reversed cards also mean no. But if you are not reading reversals, just turn the reversed cards up and refer to the list below to determine the answer to your burning question.

YES CARDS	NO CARDS	NEUTRAL CARDS	EXCEPTIONS
All cards aside from those listed in the next three columns	Swords: 3, 5, 6, 7, 8, 9, 10 Knight Cups: 5, 7, 8 Pentacles: 5 Death The Devil The Tower	Swords: 4 Cups: 4 The Hermit The Hanged Man	Ten of Wands (The answer is not yet known) Two of Swords Five and Seven of

	The Moon		Wands (The answer is yes, but you should work hard for it)

The Celtic Cross

The Celtic Cross is a popular Tarot layout that can provide you a brief insight of your present life.

Before you start, you should set your intention by asking a question as you fan out or cut the deck.

Shuffle the cards, and place them on the table as shown in the

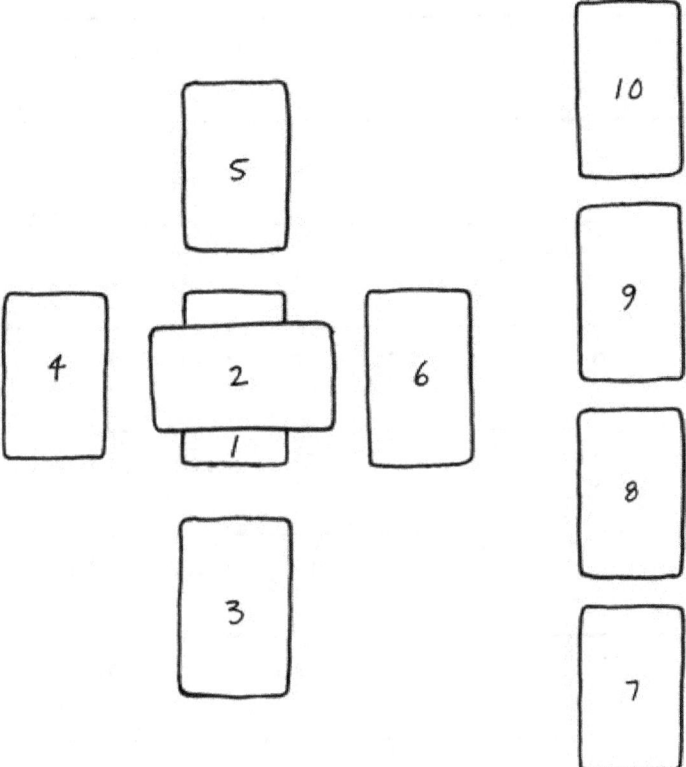

picture below:

Refer to this table in interpreting the cards in the Celtic Cross layout:

CARD NUMBER	INTERPRETATION
1	Your current position

2	Possible challenges
3	What to focus on
4	Your pas
5	Your strengths
6	Immediate future
7	Suggested solution
8	What you need to know
9	Hopes and fears
10	Your future

You may also select a random card from this layout and start a 3-card reading. Remember, if card number 10 is a court card (a King, Queen, Knight or a Page), then the result of the question relies on you or the recipient of your reading.

The Weekly Forecast

To gain insight of your week ahead, you can lay down one card for each day (not necessarily in chronological order).

You may also read the month ahead or year ahead by laying down one card for each month in sequence, starting with the present month, but in the placement of numbers in a clockwise.

You will need a Signifier card that you will place in the center, surrounded by the months of the cards. So if it is currently at September, you need to start with a September card, then October, and so on.

The Tree of Life Layout

The Tree of Life Layout is considered as an advanced Tarot layout. It can be challenging to perform, so this is usually not recommended for beginners.

But for the sake of knowledge, and so you can come back here once you are confident in your skills, we will still discuss this layout.

The primary theme of the Tree of Life is based on the Kabbalah, particularly the creation story or the sephirots. On the next page, you'll find an image that depicts this kind of layout.

Based on this story, the Divine will flow from the source, which creates the three upper sephirots that in turn created the lower sephirots.

These sephirots serve as the container of the Divine Will of creation and the pathways of the Tree of Life represents the downward flow of the Divine Will from the upper sephirot known as Kether to the lower sephirots known as Malkuth.

The meaning of each sphere or card placement is used in this layout to provide a clearer channel for using the Tarot deck as a tool for divination.

However, the layout also includes the conventional sphere interpretations that you can use if you want to gain insight on your spiritual self.

Below are the meanings of the cards if you want to use it for divination:

CARD NUMBER	INTERPRETATION
1	Your situation
2	Responsibilities
3	Limitations and the past
4	What supports you

5	What opposes you
6	Achievements
7	Attractions and relationships
8	Work, health, and communication
9	What is hidden
10	The outcome or future environment

Below are the meanings of the cards if you want to use it for spiritual insight:

CARD NUMBER	INTERPRETATION
1 (Kether)	Unity and spiritual growth
2 (Chokmah)	Wisdom, the male principle
3 (Binah)	Understanding the female

	principle
4 (Chesed)	Love, universal love, peace, and the law
5 (Geburah)	Power and destruction, judgement and negative aspects
6 (Tiphareth)	Beauty, the child, rebirth and progress
7 (Netzach)	Endurance, relationships and instinct
8 (Hod)	The mind: intelligence, creativity, communication
9 (Yesod)	The unconscious mind: intuition, mysteries, dreams
10 (Malkuth)	The environment

The Chakra Spread

This spread follows the placement of the 7 chakra positions in the body.

This layout will help you answer your questions about certain aspects of life aspects.

Here is the guide for the Chakra Layout

CARD NUMBER	INTERPRETATION
7 (Crown)	Spirituality / Life Goals
6 (Third Eye)	Trust / Intuition
5 (Throat)	Communication
4 (Heart)	Love and Relationships
3 (Solar)	Energy, health and wisdom
2 (Sacral)	Creativity and projects
1 (Root)	Finances and home security

Chapter 4. Interpreting the Major Arcana Cards

Before we take a closer look on the interpretation for each card in the Major Arcana, here is a quick-reference guide:

CARD NUMBER	CHARACTER	GENERAL INTERPRETATION
0	The Fool	Beginnings
I	The Magician	Action and ambition
II	The High Priestess	Learning, intuition, and secrets
III	The Empress	Motherhood, resources, creativity
IV	The Emperor	Power, boundaries, order
V	The Hierophant	Education, marriage, unity
VI	The Lovers	Decisions, love

VII	The Chariot	Determination, progress
VIII	Strength	Endurance, Management
IX	The Hermit	Solitude, analysis
X	The Wheel of Fortune	Fate, luck
XI	Justice	Balance, decisions, legal affairs
XII	The Hanged Man	Sacrifice, Waiting
XIII	Death	Change, transformation, new beginnings
XIV	Temperance	Negotiation
XV	The Devil	Restriction
XVI	The Tower	Illumination, Breakdown

XVII	The Star	Guidance and hope
XVIII	The Moon	Deep emotions, crisis of faith
XIX	The Sun	Recovery and growth
XX	Judgement	The past, second chances
XXI	The World	Completion, success

The Fool

Character: The Fool

Number: 0

Alternative Names: The Idiot, The Jester

Element: Air

Astrological Sign/ Planet: Uranus

Hebrew Letter: Aleph

General Interpretation: Beginnings, Risks, Innocence

The Fool is depicted as the innocent adventurer who is about to start a crucial journey. Take note of how his clothes are not fit for travel, and he looks upwards, which is a sign of being idealistic and impractical.

The Fool is accompanied by a little dog that tries to warn him of danger. However, the character ignores the warning.

The number of the Fool is zero, which symbolizes new beginnings. As he travels through the sequence of the Major Arcana, he can be considered as part of each card.

However, he also stands beyond the sequence, without any formal value. A real novice, the Fool is about to explore the world, obtain experience, and will soon leave his amateur status.

The Fool travels light, without the burden of any commitment. He is a dreamer who is guided only by his desires and needs.

Portrayed as a young man, the Fool is guided to become a mature being in the next card - the Magician who has started gaining knowledge and has already figured out some secrets to help him succeed.

Throughout his journey, the Fool will collect the four suits in the Minor Arcana - the Wand, the Pentacle, the Sword, and the Cup, which are important for his survival. The Wand is used to connect to his inner divinity, the Pentacle (coin) for material possession, the Sword to defend himself, and the Cup for drinking water (satisfaction of his body needs).

At this phase of the Fool's journey, he is yet to learn the power and meaning of these suits. Once he completely understand their essence, he may level up to the next phase of life.

The Upright Fool

When upright, the Fool denotes calculated risk. It could mean that it is never too late to start anew and follow the desires of your heart. The journey you are about to take could be dangerous, but have faith and take the leap.

The Reversed Fool

The reversed Fool denotes irresponsibility. Without considering the disadvantages of certain actions, you might make some decisions that are not wise.

The Fool leaps without any guidance and so becomes the Idiot who damages the opportunities present because of irrationality and desperation.

If this card appears on the reverse, you should be careful before you agree to a new method of work and try to hold back from any commitments until you are certain of your decision.

The Magician

Character: The Magician

Number: I

Alternative Names: The Magus, The Juggler

Element: Air

Astrological Sign/ Planet: Mercury

Hebrew Letter: Beth

General Interpretation: Success, creativity, action

The Magician in the Tarot card is in action shown with a magic wand and the suits of the deck - the Wand, the Sword, the Cup, and the Pentacle.

Using these suits, he intends to transform them to create the ether or the fifth element, which is also known as the mythical "breath of the gods".

As the next card in the sequence, the Magician was once the Fool who has now acquired great knowledge by aligning the spirit and matter.

As the mediator between heaven and earth, the Magician stands for creativity and decisions.

The flowers surrounding the character denotes that a life that is committed to a certain passion could be beautiful.

As the Magician is the successor to the Fool, as we transform from a cosmic egg to I or the individual.

The number of the Magician is I or the first prime number that signifies the primal energy. This further denotes the oneness with God or the divine spirit.

This Major Arcana card is connected to The Wheel of Fortune (X) and The Sun (XIX) because these two cards link with the consciousness of realms beyond the material world.

The Upright Magician

An upright Magician card could mean that it is time to express or communicate your desires or ideas. The Magician card is the card for the entrepreneur, the self-employed, the traveler, and the inventor as it urges the recipient of the reading to widen the current horizon.

It could signify that you will have the drive to push your plans and possibly to take new innovative approaches to let go of procrastination, trust your inner gut, ask questions, and think logically.

With your magic wand, you will have the capacity to transform your current situation, so this is usually seen as a positive card.

The Reversed Magician

The opposite of the Magician is the Trickster. So this card usually denotes that you might be fooled by a charming person.

What you are dealing now may not be the truth. It is all show. If you are currently working on a project, the reversed Magician card may show a creative block as you feel you are in the middle of two major decisions. It may be time to choose one path and completely give your commitment.

The reversed card may also signify delays in your travel plans.

The High Priestess
Character: The High Priestess

Number: II

Alternative Names: The Papess

Element: Water

Astrological Sign/ Planet: The Moon

Hebrew Letter: Gimel

General Interpretation: Spiritual world, wisdom, secrets

The High Priestess is depicted as standing in a temple or a narrow chamber between two pillars named B and J.

Behind her is a veil designed with date fruit and pomegranates. Her headdress features a horned moon that resembles the head piece of Hathor (an Egyptian goddess). A crescent moon is seen at her feet. She also holds a partly hidden scroll carrying the letters T, O, R, and A that indicates the Torah or the sacred text of the Jews.

The High Priestess symbolizes the divinity of the female character. In the past versions of early Tarot cards, this character is called the Female Pope that is portrayed as a virgin priestess in white and blue robes.

In the Rider-Waite-Smith Tarot, the High Priestess is portrayed as a spiritual teacher, astrologer, and psychic. Her spiritual journey is above earthly connections and material values.

The Upright High Priestess

The High Priestess is imbued with psychic experience, intuition, and arcane knowledge. If it appears in an upright position, it means you are in a time for privacy or incubation. Use this time to understand your inner self and nurture your relationship with your spiritual self.

Confidentiality is important in your everyday life. If you have a project you are working on or you are keeping a secret, it is better to keep them hidden.

The Reversed High Priestess

If the High Priestess appears in reverse, it signifies that you are influenced by an inappropriate guide or you are following a wrong path. You might be swayed by bad advice or someone might push you to go against your natural grain. This is also a sign that you have to divulge an important secret. The High Priestess reminds you that any knowledge that is hidden for too long could do you harm.

The Empress

Character: The Empress

Number: III

Alternative Names: The Mother

Element: Earth

Astrological Sign/ Planet: Venus

Hebrew Letter: Daleth

General Interpretation: Creativity, generosity, abundance

As the archetype of the mother identity, the Empress is the symbol of abundance and creativity.

Her shield bears the symbol of Venus linking her to the planet Venus and the Roman goddess of beauty and love.

In Roman Mythology, Venus was not only worshipped as the ruler of romantic relationships but was also considered as the nature or mother herself.

The corn growing at her feet, green trees, and the flowing river at her side suggests abundance.

Even though the Empress is living on Earth, she is still deeply rooted and has the courage to go with the flow. Her loose dress and lazy pose could mean that she is pregnant.

The Upright Empress

The Empress are endowed with emotional support, sensuality, security, material comfort and abundance.

This card is auspicious especially for mothers and children because it symbolizes femininity and fertility.

The Empress is creative and resourceful, so if this card appears in your reading, there's a high percentage that your needs in the immediate future will be satisfied.

The Reversed Empress

If reversed, the Empress could mean domestic strife and financial issues. This could take the form of disruptive problems at home. This card may also suggest a creative block in your projects or you are involved with a person who is taking too much of your resources.

The outcome of these demands and challenges are stressful. The reversed Empress may also signify that you might find it difficult to conceive a child.

The Emperor
Character: The Emperor

Number: IV

Alternative Names: The Grandfather

Element: Fire

Astrological Sign/ Planet: Aries

Hebrew Letter: Heh

General Interpretation: Ambition, security, control, order

The Emperor is the symbol of fatherhood, virility, and male dominance. His long beard signifies wisdom and maturity.

Eventually, the Emperor will become the Hermit - another character in the Tarot deck with a beard.

But while the Hermit is in isolation and idle, the Emperor is vigorous and ready to take action.

The number of the Emperor is IV, which signifies order and stability and often associated with the four directions in the compass. This character is certain of his position and as suggested in the way he sits in the throne.

His mountainous background seem to support him and protect him. But he is seen as higher than the mountains, which suggest that he is control.

The Upright Emperor

The Emperor discloses control and mastery of life. When appears upright, it could mean that you can overcome current life challenges through single mindedness and careful planning.

This card signifies stability, so the presence of this card into your reading is a good sign of progress in your current circumstance. You can also trust in your decision making skills or someone you trust will help you.

The Emperor urges you to live in the present and use the available resources at your disposal to achieve your goals.

The Reversed Emperor

In reverse, the Emperor represents the negative aspects of masculinity like cruelty, being too controlling, and dominance.

Excessive demands and greed are other aspects of Emperor when reversed.

While the upright card suggests that you are aware of your limitations, the reversed card may signify that you are not paying attention of your boundaries. You might be using excessive force in achieving your goals.

Therefore, a reversed Emperor card shows potential problems with authority.

The Hierophant

Character: The Hierophant

Number: V

Alternative Names: The Pope, The High Priest

Element: Earth

Astrological Sign/ Planet: Taurus

Hebrew Letter: Vau

General Interpretation: Spiritual direction, unity, education

The Hierophant is portrayed as an image of religious orthodoxy. Holding the scepter and wearing the papal crown, he also gives his blessing to two supplicants before him.

Originally known as the Pope, one of his titles is The Great Bridge Builder because he serves as the bridge between earth and heaven.

This card is also a symbol of education. He is named after the *hierophantes* or the priests who tended to the Elyssian Fields. Through this character, you are reminded that you can find a higher path through learning.

The Upright Hierophant

In upright position, the Hierophant signifies expansion, self-realization, and support. If you get this card, it could mean that it is time to develop your spiritual and emotional self.

You may need to be more aware of your spiritual self, to give more time for introspection, and to nurture your personal relationships.

The Hierophant provides you an opportunity to integrate your spirt and mind, so you can ascend to a higher level of consciousness.

The Reversed Hierophant

If reversed, the Hierophant signifies poor leadership. Your current leader at work or on your spiritual journey might be incompetent or egotistic.

The reversed Hierophant is the card of bad master - the selfish guru who is more interested in advancing his goals than supporting you.

At work, the reverse Hierophant may also show organizations that are in need of restructuring. It may be best to find your own path than to stay with your current mentor or organization that is not satisfying your needs.

The Hierophant urges you to be a free spirit.

The Lovers
Character: The Lovers

Number: VI

Alternative Names: Love, the Lover

Element: Air

Astrological Sign/ Planet: Gemini

Hebrew Letter: Zain

General Interpretation: Love and relationships, decisions, maturity

This card portrays the two lovers in a magical garden with the full sun beaming behind Archangel Raphael.

The man - who is suspected to be the Fool portrayed in the first card - looks directly at the woman who in turn looks up towards the luminous angel.

The clouds between the lovers predict the challenges they will overcome as they become more familiar with each other.

The Upright Lovers

The Lovers card predicts that you are about to meet a new partner or you will be offered a new opportunity for your career. Your choice in the coming days will have an important impact on your future.

If this card appears in your reading in an upright position, the person that you will meet in the near future will have a positive influence and provide you with true love as long as you listen to your heart instead of your mind.

If you are currently in a relationship, you may need to make a decision if you want to take this in a deeper level.

Regardless of your situation, the message of the Lovers is to listen to the desires of your heart. If you are a young person, you may soon find yourself leaving home so you can pursue your own dreams.

The Reversed Lovers

If the Lovers card appears reversed, your relationships may go out of balance. Your relationship may be in crisis and you may doubt your initial feelings as the common things you have before seem no longer there.

The reversed arrival of this card could mean dishonesty, betrayal, and inequality. It is also a component of XV card or the Devil that reveals materialism and lust.

The Chariot
Character: The Chariot

Number: VII

Alternative Names: Victory

Element: Water

Astrological Sign/ Planet: Cancer

Hebrew Letter: Heth

General Interpretation: Journey, victory, determination

The Chariot is a strong traveler who stands strong in his stone carriage and flanked by two great sphinxes.

He appears to travel from the city signifying self-control and determination. He has the skills to keep his carriage on the road and be successful.

At this phase, the man shown in the card is focused on the practical concerns instead of the magical. However, he is still conscious of the divine realms as shown by the astrological symbols on his belt and his astral canopy.

The Upright Chariot

The upright Chariot card usually signifies success. If you get this card, you might be in a time that you need to focus as you journey in a new pathway.

You have probably made up your mind and now you can start you experience real progress in your career. Ready to take the reins and explore your path, you are in a good position to learn as you expand your progress.

A more trivial prediction would be that you may find yourself getting a new car soon.

The Reversed Chariot

When reversed, the Chariot card signifies self-indulgence and arrogance. It may also predict that you or a person close to your may spiral out of control.

Selfishness is at play and ego comes first than greater good. Therefore, the reversed Chariot may indicate poor leadership and recklessness.

Strength
Character: Strength

Number: VIII

Alternative Names: Force, Fortitude

Element: Fire

Astrological Sign/ Planet: Leo

Hebrew Letter: Teth

General Interpretation: Strength, tension, patience

Strength is one of the four cardinal virtues featured in the Major Arcana sequence.

This Tarot card shows a curious portrayal of strength - a maiden calmly holding the jaws of a lion. The lady is in control by holding her position, as symbolized by the infinity symbol on her crown.

She signifies civility, while the lion is the symbol for base instincts and passion. By nature, the lion is an extremely dangerous animal. But the lady is not afraid.

Her calm presence influences the lion without denying his strength. Through this, the Strength card tells us to be courageous in listening and accepting our emotions.

The Upright Strength

The upright Strength card signifies that you have the ability to tune into your inner divinity for self-guidance. This means that you can easily overcome any challenge or pressure that you are about to experience.

You need to be patient, determined, and courageous as this is the best time gain control of the situation. You need to respond with sensitivity and grace instead of using force.

This is a positive card for leaders as it is a sign that you are ready to stand your ground and take on new challenges.

The Reversed Strength

The presence of the reversed Strength card in your reading signifies weakness of will and avoidance of making decisions, risks, and conflicts.

This could mean that you are ignoring your instincts or you are letting your fear of risk to stop you from taking any action.

This trait may hold back your personal progress, and in this situation, you may learn something useful.

Bear in mind that a reversed Strength card is a clear sign of weakness. Overthinking and indolence can drain you than actually tackling on your problems.

The Hermit
Character: The Hermit

Number: IX

Alternative Names: The Poor Man, Time, The old Man

Element: Earth

Astrological Sign/ Planet: Virgo

Hebrew Letter: Yod

General Interpretation: Self-exploration, healing

The Hermit card depicts a bearded old man in isolation. He only has a staff and a lantern to accompany him in the winter wilderness.

If you take a look at his lantern, you can see a luminous star that serves as a symbol that illuminates his path. In order to think and plan, the Hermit requires silence and time.

The Hermit might be travelling in a snowy wilderness, but this environment is crucial to him. Through this depiction, the Hermit card tells you that it might be the perfect time to break free from conventions so you can find your own path.

The Upright Hermit

You may need to take a break for a while so you can look at your options or pursue a personal project. The Hermit card might be telling you to enjoy solitude, because you need the space to process your thoughts.

While the Hermit card shows a physical journey, he represents a state of mind in which you detach from yourself. It also shows non-conforming to conventions and searching for a creative approach to a problem.

The Hermit is also associated with healing, so this card may indicate that you are in the process of self-healing or you will play an important role in healing others.

The Reversed Hermit

The reversed Hermit card indicates that you feel unsupported and alone. But this is more mindset than actual reality. Hence, you must ask yourself if you are ignoring the availability of assistance.

This may also predict accepting a role - possibly a martyr or a victim - that you find difficult to let go because of sheer stubbornness or mere habit.

This card may also reflect that you are currently cut off from your regular support systems or you are having a fall out with your trusted friends.

The Wheel of Fortune

Character: The Wheel of Fortune

Number: X

Alternative Names: The Wheel, Destiny, Fate

Element: Fire

Astrological Sign/ Planet: Jupiter

Hebrew Letter: Kaph

General Interpretation: Intuition, change, fate

Flanked by winged figure and three animals, the Wheel of Fortune appears in the sky in the midst of the clouds. This signifies spiritual breakthrough, clarity, and hope.

Divine law is in action with the Wheel of Fortune in effect. This card is number X, which marks the mid-point in the Major Arcana sequence. From this point, we are now turning to the external phase that views our relationship with the external world to another phase that starts our inner, spiritual journey.

The Upright Wheel of Fortune

The upright presence of this card signifies positive outcome. Good news, unexpected career offers, and significant meetings will happen in the near future.

If your life has been challenging lately, this card promises a better turn. Under this influence, your powerful intuition will significantly improve, and you may find yourself tuning in to people from your past.

The Reversed Wheel of Fortune

The reversed Wheel usually signifies bad luck. But despite this, you will find relief that this is also a sign that your challenges will soon come to an end.

Through this, the basic interpretation of this Wheel is closure. The promises of the upright card will still arrive but may just take a bit while.

On a spiritual level, this card may also signify that you don't trust your intuition. Listen to your inner voice so you can keep on progressing towards your goal.

Justice

Character: Justice

Number: XI

Alternative Names: Adjustment

Element: Air

Astrological Sign/ Planet: Libra

Hebrew Letter: Lamed

General Interpretation: Objectivity, perception, balance

The Justice card portrays the judge or the personification of Justice holding the symbols of low - the scales and the upright sword. But unlike the conventional figures of justice, the figure in this card is not blindfolded. She has a clear vision.

Justice is in favor of those who deserve the virtue but is ready to seek retribution for wrongdoings. She is focused on delivering logical procedures and focused on the mind instead of the emotions.

While Justice is enrobed in red (signifying the material world) the yellow background of the card suggest enlightenment. The design of the card is strikingly similar to the High Priestess and the Hierophant that points out to knowledge and duality.

Justice is one of the four cardinal virtues of the Tarot (the other virtues are Prudence, Temperance, and Strength).

But take note that the Prudence card has disappeared from the Tarot, but its meaning is seen as associated in Justice. Instead of caution, prudence is seen as wisdom. The study of law is called jurisprudence.

The Upright Justice

The upright Justice card signifies a positive outcome. The time is near when imbalances or past errors will be redressed. You will be the recipient of a fair system as long as you are deserving and honest.

Also, you might find yourself as the judge of your own life using your integrity and perspective to make sound decisions that will protect your future.

You may also take a moral stand on the issue, which affects you and the people you care about. If you are currently involved in a legal issue, a ruling or decision made will be in your favor. Order will be restored and justice will be done.

The Reversed Justice

Your life may be out of balance. Money and relationship issues spiral out of control. A ruling may go against you so there might be a miscarriage of justice or dishonesty.

You are unfairly treated that is compounded by malevolent advice from a trusted authority. You may find it difficult to speak your truth. The reversed Justice card encourages you to find your voice and keep your principles if you know you are right.

The Hanged Man
Character: The Hanged Man

Number: XII

Alternative Names: The Traitor

Element: Water

Astrological Sign/ Planet: Neptune

Hebrew Letter: Mem

General Interpretation: Enlightenment, sacrifice, waiting

At first glance, the image of a man hanging from a tree can be negative. But if you examine his face, you will see that he is calm even beatific. He is portrayed with a halo even though he hangs by one leg.

The man in this card is hanging on a tree instead of a scaffold. This tree is the Tree of Life, which is the symbol of esoteric world, even though the tree is still young and signifies future possibilities.

It is certain that the Hanged Man is not facing death. Instead, he is just "hanging around" until his situation changes.

The Upright Hanged Man

The upright Hanged Man may reflect the events in your life not moving with speed. All you might do today is to patiently wait in the knowledge that the universe has its plan.

This card may also signify that you have made recent sacrifices and you are excited to see the results. But it will be impossible to force the outcome that is within your time frame.

There are numerous other factors about which you can have no influence or know-how. Thus, you may also see some delays in your projects or travel plans.

Another message from this card is to try to see things from a new perspective. If your approach is not working, try to ask yourself if you can find a way to turn the situation around.

The Reversed Hanged Man

The Reversed Hanged Man can be a sign of martyrdom and rigid thinking. You may have to reframe your mind. What you think you want may not be possible.

The reversed arrival of this card encourages you to think a closer look at you plans. There is a possibility that you are hanging on to a fantasy that you are a victim instead of a victor.

Take another perspective and free yourself from an obligation or a contract that cannot satisfy your needs.

Death
Character: Death

Number: XIII

Alternative Names: Thirteen, Transformation, Mortality

Element: Water

Astrological Sign/ Planet: Scorpio

Hebrew Letter: Nun

General Interpretation: Change, transformation

A skeletal figure riding a horse - the personification of Death - reminds us of our frailties. However, the Death card in the Tarot deck is not a sign of your imminent demise. Instead, this card predicts a significant change in your life.

As a reaper, Death brings in harvest that is portrayed by the ears of corn shown in his flag. Whatever is irrelevant will be taken and whatever is worth will be saved.

Death affects everyone, regardless of status as depicted by the people on the card at different stages of surrender or death from the maiden to the king from the child to the bishop.

The Upright Death

When upright, the Death card reflects your current situation as a time of deep transformation. This might be your chance to free yourself from anything that you no longer need.

The impact of this card might be shocking and sudden. You may have minimal control when Death arrives. But in time, you might be able to see this important change in circumstances as a blessing.

There are times that the only way forward is to break from the past. Let go of relationships or practices that no longer satisfy your needs. As such, Death could bring relief. After all, Death is the ultimate reality check that could leave you with the truth.

The Reversed Death

The reversed Death card has virtually the same meaning as the card in upright presence. The difference could be in how you respond to change. Instead of being accepting, you may feel stressed or anxious or unable to understand what is happening.

When Death is reversed, the universe might be telling you that there's no way back - a person you are persuading will not change his or her mind or a tarnished relationship cannot be mended.

This card also signals final confirmation if you perform a second reading and you ask the question again and this card appears.

Temperance

Character: Temperance

Number: XIV

Alternative Names: Art

Element: Fire

Astrological Sign/ Planet: Sagittarius

Hebrew Letter: Samekh

General Interpretation: Angelic guidance, healing, reconciliation, moderation

The Temperance card portrays an angel holding two cups with flowing water. His right foot is on the water (present) and his left foot is on the rock (past).

There is also a clear path that runs from the pool through the mountains moving towards a foreseeable future - a bright rising sun.

A new perspective or horizon can be seen. The riverbank is verdant and lush, and two yellow flowers are present, which is a symbol of hope.

The angel of temperance controls the water flow creating harmony.

The Upright Temperance

You may need to handle a sensitive situation, and you have to control your actions and thoughts to preserve harmony and balance. Chances are, you may need to blend two opposing forces to build an inspired solution.

Temperance also asks you not to resist, but also accept the two sides of a situation and be guided by what feels natural to you. This could be the perfect time for reconciliation.

This angelic card may also signify that you are being guided with angels or your spiritual guides. Expect for an illuminating advice from a close friend or even a stranger whom the angels sent to assist you.

The Reversed Temperance

The reversed arrival of the Temperance card signifies unfairness and disharmony in relationships as well as financial problems. What are you pouring into your work or into your relationship is not rewarded.

This card also reflects struggle with change and the past dominating your future and present. In your current position, painful memories of the past may surface again and you feel trapped. Try to refocus yourself in the present.

The Devil
Character: Devil

Number: XV

Alternative Names: Temptation, Pan

Element: Earth

Astrological Sign/ Planet: Capricorn

Hebrew Letter: Ayin

General Interpretation: Temptation, enslavement

The Devil card shows a bearded creature sitting on top of a door that chains two demons - a male and a female.

With the inverted pentacle on his crown, the man-beast is clearly the devil. His right hand is raised signifying that he has control over the two demons standing before him. These two figures are the Lovers who have lost their way. They have been corrupted and so they are becoming evil.

But if you take a closer look, the chains around their necks are not that tight. They are not completely dominated by the devil, and they can easily walk away if they want to.

The Upright Devil

You might be following a path or you might be in a relationship, which demands too much. What began positively or even pleasurably has now reversed, and now you see the situation for what it is.

This is a damaging situation, and you might feel controlled and under a bad influence. The Devil card is a card of materialism, temptation, and greed.

But to change your situation, you have to think creatively and use a bit of wit. The negativity is too high so it may be best not to confront the situation altogether. This card usually appears when you are in a situation that you can't fix. Its message is to just walk away, escape in the best way you can no matter how good the offer.

Other meanings of the Devil card are related to addiction such as substance abuse, food, sex and other damaging habits.

The Reversed Devil

The reversed arrival of the Devil card brings hope because this signifies that the decision you need to make will be easier than it appears.

If the Devil card is upside down in your reading, the chains around you are more loose so a situation is not quite as problematic as you first though. This is the time to make an action.

The Tower

Character: The Tower

Number: XVI

Alternative Names: The Lightning, Fate, The House of God

Element: Fire

Astrological Sign/ Planet: Mars

Hebrew Letter: Peh

General Interpretation: Enlightenment, Destruction

This Tarot card depicts a tower being hit by lightning causing it to burn and throwing two figures out.

There is also a crown being toppled from the Tower as nature asserts its power over the Earth.

In the early version of the Tarot deck, this card is called the House of God, which is alluded to the Tower of Babel.

As with other supposedly negative cards in the Tarot deck (Devil and Death) there is also a way to move things forward with the Tower as long as we accept a higher force and mend our ways.

If you have been living mightily in a "tower" this is the time to come down and reconcile with your roots.

The Upright Tower

The upright Tower signifies that you are about to face a sudden change - in you relationships, in your work, in your goals. This is unavoidable as it is already destined by fate.

At present, you may feel confused and vulnerable as the Tower represents shattered ego. However, you may only surrender to this higher power and accept the huge shift in awareness that it brings - even though the benefits may not be clear yet.

The Reversed Tower

You may find yourself fulfilling an obligation even if you are not responsible. This may also signify that you have held on to a relationship, career, or project that has weak foundation.

Your fears could become real if you have clung to the past to protect yourself from reality. You cannot prevent the collapse of the Tower, so don't feel responsible for the forces that are outside your control. Its effect is dramatic and fast.

The Star
Character: The Star

Number: XVII

Alternative Names: The Stars, Hope

Element: Air

Astrological Sign/ Planet: Aquarius

Hebrew Letter: Tzaddi

General Interpretation: Creativity, inspiration, guidance, hope

In tune with the world, the maiden portrayed in the Star card is naked signifying truth and purity. While she is rooted to the Earth, he is also associated with the divine.

Above the maiden are eight stars with the guiding star a lot bigger than the others.

The Upright Star

The Star card reveals guidance and hope. So if you have been struggling lately, this card is a positive sign that your luck will soon change for the better.

This card is a powerful symbol of hope, and you will soon learn how to appreciate everything in life including spiritual and physical well-being. The Star is a supporter of creativity and aesthetics as reflected by the flowing water in the card.

In your relationships and projects, you can be completely expressed, sharing your talents, gifts, and love. You will soon shine and your hard work will be appreciated. Your insight and intuition will also improve under the influence of the Star.

The Reversed Star

When reversed, the Start signifies a creative block or your tendency to give up early on a project. You might be too attached in the fantasy realm and you might be ignoring the details.

As an alternative, you might feel lulled into a false sense of security in a business that has no strong foundation and minimal chance of success. You may also feel alone now, without the support that you need.

The Moon

Character: The Moon

Number: XVIII

Alternative Names: Luna, Illusion

Element: Water

Astrological Sign/ Planet: Pisces

Hebrew Letter: Kuf

General Interpretation: Crisis, dreams, illusion

The Moon card signifies emotional turmoil and duality with the symbolism of two howling dogs and towers.

One dog is a wolf while the other is domesticated. This represents the duality of inner conflict.

While this card is named the Moon, it portrays a sun-moon that seems to gaze at the earth but notice that the eyes are closed. This signifies that the perspective of daylight is blind under the light of the moon.

The crayfish at the bottom of the card seems to struggle between the land and water. This means something important is about to happen. The crayfish reflects your fears.

Like the crayfish you must make a decision so you can resolve the conflict between taking the challenge of the unknown or staying in a safe place.

The Upright Moon

The conventional interpretation of the Moon card is a crisis of faith and a time of emotional turmoil. This reflects your doubt about a situation as you are not certain if what you see is real.

Under the moonlight try to see if what you see is an illusion. Or does the light of the moon bring light the core of a problem that requires your attention. This could be a time of emotional conflict that you are hiding.

You need to make a decision. However, you have to trust your senses instead of logic.

Be aware of your intuition and dreams now as significant signs to guide you to the right path. You may need to journey into the unknown, but this card encourages you to deep dive and take a closer look on the actual cause of your troubles.

The Reversed Moon

If the Moon is reversed, you may need to stay away from difficult confrontations and emotions. Hence, your needs are not recognized or expressed.

You are ignoring a trauma instead of exploring it. So, the reversed Moon card may show you going back to your old habits of handling problems. The card also suggests that you feel trapped in an old emotional pattern that keeps on recurring.

The Sun
Character: The Sun

Number: XIX

Alternative Name: The Children

Element: Fire

Astrological Sign/ Planet: The Sun

Hebrew Letter: Resh

General Interpretation: Good health, success

The Sun card depicts the cosmic light. The child riding the horse suggests that he is ready to return home.

He is full of joy and his nakedness is the symbol of innocence. The Sun card is one of the most positive Tarot cards signifying happiness, success, and growth.

The Upright Sun

If you have been struggling recently, the Sun card shows that your situation will improve son. You will be the recipient of cosmic energy, so you will be filled with life to face the days ahead.

This card also predicts return to good health if you or someone close to you has suffered from health concerns.

As a positive card, all your projects will be successful. The Sun heralds a great time to rekindle your creative projects, your career and the people who really matters to you.

If this appears with a negative card, the Sun has the dominating power to counter the bad prediction.

The Reversed Sun

The Sun has no negative sides even if it arrives in your reading in reverse. The only problem could be a delay to your travel arrangements. However, you will still benefit from positive outcomes.

Judgement
Character: Judgement

Number: XX

Alternative Names: Time, Fame, The Angel

Element: Fire

Astrological Sign/ Planet: Pluto

Hebrew Letter: Shin

General Interpretation: Letting go of the past, assessment

This Tarot card portrays Judgement Day, which was prophesied by St. Paul. The archangel would blow a trumpet to awaken the souls of the departed so they will be judged by God.

The angel in this card is Gabriel, and his trumpet signals a call for revelation when you can learn the truth. You may also be awakened to a new relationship to the divine with your angel.

This card is one of the three cards that depict an angel (the other cards are Temperance and Love).

The Upright Judgement

Now is the time to make a decision about your past. Great opportunities will come but you need to be clear on your direction. You must address specific issues in the past.

The process is completely about how you judge yourself on your previous actions and attitudes. The upright appearance of this card shows you have acted with integrity and you have done your best.

It is also the time to toot your own horn and be proud of yourself for your accomplishments.

The Reversed Judgement

You might be stuck in the past or you are resisting to learn the valuable lessons presented to you. You feel that you are trapped by your old habits or negative thinking patterns.

Delays are also shown and you may be feeling trapped or unable to progress without really understanding the core details. You are capable of assessing your attitudes and actions and then move one. Accept the past and understand the person you were then and for the decisions you had to make.

It is time to be free.

The World
Character: The World

Number: XXI

Alternative Names: The Universe

Element: Earth

Astrological Sign/ Planet: Saturn

Hebrew Letter: Tau

General Interpretation: Joy, reward, success, completion

The World is one of the most positive cards in the Tarot deck. It signifies completion and success.

This card portrays a maiden holding a wand in each hand and encircled by an oval laurel wreath.

The World maiden is protected by the four figures that can also be seen in the Wheel of Fortune card. These figures are the symbols of the four gospel evangelists.

The figure in the center is also the Fool. From his early beginnings, he has journeyed throughout the world and now ready for rebirth. While the figure is clearly a maiden, it is believed that the fabric hides the male genitals of the Fool. This suggests the perfect balance of opposites - the male and female or the sun and moon.

The Upright World

You will soon see completion of your projects and reap the rewards for your efforts. As such, the upright appearance of the World card is one of the happiest readings in the card.

This card signifies happiness and deep joy and now you can really feel that you deserve success. You will be popular for completed projects, but your life is in harmony.

The Reversed World

You are ready to let go and move on but you feel you don't deserve success. It may also show hanging on to a dream that has been eluding you. You may need to reassess what you want and adjust your expectations.

Just like the Sun card, the negative energy brought by the reversed World card are minor. In the end, you will soon get what you deserve. It may take a while, but have faith.

Chapter 5. Interpreting Minor Arcana Cards: The Suit Of Wands

CARD	MEANING
King of Wands	A creative man
Queen of Wands	A creative woman
Knight of Wands	An offer
Page of Wands	A message
Ten of Wands	A burden
Nine of Wands	Strength
Eight of Wands	News
Seven of Wands	Advocacy
Six of Wands	Victory
Five of Wands	Strong opinion
Four of Wands	A holiday

Three of Wands	Travel
Two of Wands	Making Plans
Ace of Wands	Beginnings, male fertility

The King of Wands

Character: The King of Wands

Element: Air of the suit of Fire

Astrological Sign/ Planet: Cancer and Leo

General Interpretation: An honorable man

The King of Wands is associated with the Emperor or the symbol of father image who brings authority, order and structure.

His robe and throne are designed with black salamanders, who are resistant to fire. There's also a live salamander at the bottom of the card, which reinforces the King of Wand as a fire suit. The card is also dominated by orange and red that signifies passion and ambition.

The Upright King of Wands

This is the best time to express your ideas and collect your entrepreneurial spirit. Build a plan and the ideas you will pursue have higher chances of success. You will have all the support that you need, but you need to initiate the plan.

Just do it. Avoid over thinking and don't allow perfectionism to impede your ability to achieve your goals.

Here are the interpretations if you get two or more Kings in your reading:

> Two Kings - a viable partnership
>
> Three Kings - circle of influence
>
> Four Kings - a battle for power

The Reversed King of Wands

You are in a time of restriction when you can't convince others to support your ideas. Try checking if you are not going against your intuition, especially if you feel that you are not in the right path. Be open to alternative ways and stop pressuring yourself too much.

The Queen of Wands
Character: The Queen of Wands

Element: Water of the suit of Fire

Astrological Sign/ Planet: Aries and Pisces

General Interpretation: Focus and creativity

The Queen of Wands is associated with the Empress and also a symbol of motherhood representing the soul.

Similar to the Magician, this Queen manifests her ideas for the spiritual path. Her wand is alive and it is her job to nurture this wood. She also holds a sunflower, which is a solar symbol for illumination, growth, and energy.

The Upright Queen of Wands

Ideas thrive, and you can now express your abilities. Show your true self and fire up your passion. But you also need to reflect how you are managing your life to ensure that you have the time to grab the opportunities that are coming your way.

In general, this card shows you are strong to nurture your career, family, friendships, and romance.

If there are two or more Queens during your reading, it can be interpreted in the following ways:

> Two Queens: Rivalry
>
> Three Queens: Friends happy to help
>
> Four Queens: Women meeting up

The Reversed Queen of Wands

You need to fix something that has been messed up by someone else. This might be because you allow yourself to be in a relationship or a commitment in which this person has been taking too much but is not responsible enough.

The reversed appearance of the Queen of Wands may also signify that someone is envious of you because you are shining brighter.

The Knight of Wands
Character: The Knight of Wands

Element: Fire of the suit of Fire

Astrological Sign/ Planet: Scorpio and Sagittarius

General Interpretation: A proposal

This Minor Arcana card features a flamboyant knight riding a horse in the desert near the pyramids.

The knight is full of vigor and he holds a wand eager to deliver a message. The Knight of Wand card is an element of Fire in the suit of Fire.

Double fire signifies desire, ambition, and passion. However, the picture has no sense of imminent battle, danger, or chaos.

The reins of the horse are tight and short that at first glance provides the impression that the horse is dancing. The young Knight has control over the natural urges of the animal and knows when to hold back and when to let loose.

The Upright Knight of Wands

Things will speed up. Any hindrances to any progress will be lifted, so this is a positive card if you have been feeling trapped or if you have been waiting for decisions.

Now you can have the action and conversations you need to push forward with your projects. This card is particularly auspicious for professional projects, finding new career, or moving house.

If you get two or more Knights in a reading, the interpretations are as follows:

> Two Knights - Righteous friendship but rivalry if one or both cards are reversed
>
> Three Knights - Meeting of men
>
> Four Knights - Events speed up, lots of action

The Reversed Knight of Wands

The reversed Knight of Wands signify miscommunication. Be careful in sending a message and make sure that it is clear with both the sender and the receiver.

It also predicts delays so be ready to be disappointed with the lack of progress. But this is only temporary and will just pass. Host on to your plans and just believe in yourself.

The Page of Wands
Character: The Page of Wands

Element: Earth of the suit of Fire

General Interpretation: Communication and good news

This card portrays a young man looking upwards towards his wand. The red feather in his hat looks like a flame associating with the element of Fire signifying ambition.

The wand is taller than the man, which means that his ideas are bigger than his experience. However, he is motivated to overcome shortcomings with his enthusiasm and knowledge.

The Upright Page of Wands

The appearance of this card in a reading brings great news about projects and any situation that is in need of negotiation.

Phone calls, urgent emails, and messages will keep your schedule full, so you need to step back for a while before you react and study just how much work you have to do.

This card also predicts a job offer or a creative enterprise. While the status of the job may not be as high as you want, this opportunity will bring you more rewards in the long run.

The interpretations are as follows when two or more Pages appear in your reading:

>Two Pages - Righteous friendship

>Three Pages – Plenty of social activity

>Four Pages – A gathering of young people

The Reversed Page of Wands

If reversed, the Page of Wands signify delays. Communications can be difficult as emails and other messages go astray. Having one or multiple page cards reversed could indicate rivalry.

This may also suggest that you are at the moment showing stubbornness. Try to listen to the opinions of other people.

Ten of Wands

Character: Ten of Wands

Element: Fire

Astrological Sign/ Planet: Saturn in Sagittarius

General Interpretation: Responsibilities, burden

This card depicts a young man walking towards a manor despite his view being blocked by the wands.

There's a sense of desperation in this card because of the mystery behind the man's decision to pursue this kind of journey.

He chooses to carry the wands in front of his face that blocks his view. Possibly he sees himself not as a human but a blind beast that is desperate to be relieved from his burden.

The Upright Ten of Wands

You have too much on your shoulders right now. Over the years, you might have become so familiar with too much work that you have already missed the reason why you are working.

This is a common card for entrepreneurs, home makers, and people who are constantly multitasking or juggling different projects.

You need to learn how to delegate and ask support from the people around you. There is no need to carry all burdens on your own. This is also true for emotional burdens. You have to share them.

This card also suggests that you may be carrying issues from the past. But this also reveals that you are poised for success, even though you have to manage your time and resources well.

The Reversed Ten of Wands

The interpretation for the reversed ten of wands is quite similar to the upright card, except that some of your burdens are more physical than emotional.

This card may signify an ongoing stress, where each task is framed as a potential problem. Try to lighten up a bit and take some of the stress off yourself. No one expects you to be perfect.

This also suggests that you are sandwiched in a draining routine between domestic and work commitments because you are trying to please everyone.

Have some space for your needs. You also need to make yourself happy. Once you do this, you will see the path more clearly.

Nine of Wands

Character: Nine of Wands

Element: Fire

Astrological Sign/ Planet: Moon in Sagittarius

General Interpretation: Strength and Defense

This card portrays a wounded yet alert man. The eight standing wands symbolizes his responsibilities but also resources, and he holds the ninth wand like a tool for defense.

The other eight wands are orderly as if ready for any attack.

The man has a powerful build, which symbolizes his endurance and strength. From experience, he has learned to anticipate challenges to his position, and his previous battles are signified by the bandage on his head.

The Upright Nine of Wands

You are in a very formidable position. You have fought hard and long to obtain your status, and you have endured extreme challenges.

It can be exhausting to be constantly ingenious and vigilant, so you need to be careful in using your energy. Plan all your activities and avoid overexerting too much.

Fortunately, as with all lesser cards in the Tarot deck, the influence of this card is only temporary. There is no need to always defend yourself or make numerous sacrifices.

The Reversed Nine of Wands

You are enduring a strong opposition that seems not fair. You are working hard but you are not receiving any appreciation at all. You might be giving your all, but it seems not enough.

Your current situation might be demotivating, so you become fixed on getting through tasks without enjoying the elements of your work that you find satisfying.

Eight of Wands

Character: Eight of Wands

Element: Fire

Astrological Sign/ Planet: Mercury in Sagittarius

General Interpretation: Travel and news

This card shows eight wands with budding greens flying through a clear sky.

This is quite a special card because it is one of the only two lesser cards that don't portray people (the other one of the Three of Swords).

The interpretation of this card focuses on movement. The events are about to speed up.

The wands may be spears about to land or they may be carrying messages similar to carrier pigeons.

The wands take up most of the space of the card, which dominates everything in the picture.

The Upright Eight of Wands

This card is one of the most welcoming cards of the suit of wands. The wands predict communication so be ready to be inundated with exciting offers, calls, or emails.

The appearance of this card also suggest positive news, which is great if you are stuck waiting for decisions or if you have held back recently. Your projects will speed up so be prepared for the shift. The following events will energize you but you have to prioritize your offers.

The Reversed Eight of Wands

The reversed interpretation of this card is 'delay'. You may need to wait a bit longer for a particular decision that will lead you to a better path. But this is temporary so be patient. You may also need to work on a lot of pending tasks.

Seven of Wands
Character: Seven of Wands

Element: Earth

Astrological Sign/ Planet: Mars in Leo

General Interpretation: Challenges, effort, and courage

It is interesting to take note of the scale of this card. A young man seems a giant if you take a closer look at the landscape below.

Towering over the river and hills below, the young man is clearly not from this world.

Using his two hands, he is using everything to defend his position. He is capable of looking at the bigger picture due to his size. He has great ideas signified by the five buds on his wands in comparison with the fewer buds shown on other cards.

The other six wands are rising towards him, but the young man is ready to take them all.

The Upright Seven of Wands

There are some obstacles in your path, but you are capable of overcoming them. This card reflects your work and career and signifies negotiations regardless of how difficult the conversation becomes. You have to keep talking and stay engaged until you are happy with the result. You must hold your ground so you can win.

The Reversed Seven of Wands

The reversed arrival of this card shows that you have doubts on your purpose. People around you may not be listening to what you say and you have to overcome a lot of challenges. This card also reflects hesitation and anxiety.

Six of Wands
Character: Six of Wands

Element: Fire

Astrological Sign/ Planet: Jupiter in Leo

General Interpretation: Victory

This card depicts a young man riding a white horse and parading in victory.

He is wearing a laurel wreath, which is a symbol of power and victory. His wand also hangs the same symbol. However, the wand in this presentation symbolizes fertility, of dreams becoming reality.

Other young people are also carrying wands. They support the homecoming of a hero. One person is facing away from the hero suggesting that he is protecting the rider.

The Upright Six of Wands

You deserve whatever success you are enjoying now. This is a positive card if you have been recently struggling with your work and you are not certain that it will finally pay off.

This card is usually associated to projects, career, and work and may show promotion and a new contract or bid.

Just enjoy this happy time and do not be afraid to share your accomplishments. Other will support you. It is high time to bask in glory and celebrate with your friends.

The Reversed Six of Wands

Unfortunately, if this card appears in reverse, the reward that you are expecting will not materialize when you need it.

However, this is only a delay and not cancellation. Hold fast to your goals. Waiting for the fruits of your labor may be disappointing, but this is caused by circumstances that are beyond your control and not a reflection of your abilities.

Be patient and work on your other tasks in the meantime.

Five of Wands

Character: Five of Wands

Element: Fire

Astrological Sign/ Planet: Saturn in Leo

General Interpretation: Debate, competition

The Five of Wands portray five young men each holding a wan and at odds against each other.

They are not united as a group so they are not accomplishing anything.

Each one is focused on his own agenda: one holds his wand over his shoulder trying to keep his ambition for himself, another one holds his wand in triumph, while the other three seems battling with each other.

These young men are actually the Pages of the four minor arcana suits - brown and green (Pages of Wands), blue (Page of Pentacles), red (Page of Swords) and blue and white (Page of Cups).

The Upright Five of Wands

The traditional interpretation of the Five of Wands is competition, and this card urges you to hold your position instead of entering into a compromise.

While this card does not predict outright battle, there will be fiery expression of opinions and you may not enter into an agreement at this point.

There will be a lot of misunderstanding, especially at work.

The Reversed Five of Wands

There is misinformation and deception. You may act because someone is misleading you. Check the sources of information before you make assumptions or take any action. This card also suggests dishonesty or legal problem. Be careful of the people you trust.

Four of Wands
Character: Four of Wands

Element: Fire

Astrological Sign/ Planet: Venus in Aries

General Interpretation: Domestic happiness, creativity, freedom

One of the happiest cards of the Minor Arcana, the Four of Wands portray a celebration.

A young couple stands in victory, holding up flowers. The Four of Wands hold the garland with pink blooms, purple grapevines, plums, apples, and lemons.

This picture may show a wedding, a public holiday, or harvest time.

The bright yellow background of the card signifies solar energy, which is the power of the sun to nurture living things. Solar yellow is also the symbol of awareness that is reflected by the couple presenting themselves in public.

The Upright Four of Wands

This heartwarming card reveals success after completion. In social settings, you will have the chance to celebrate and really enjoy yourself. This card predicts that you will be brimming with vitality and confidence.

People around you will also become aware of your existence as a pillar of your workplace or home. Your talents will be appreciated and you are full of enthusiasm or ideas.

The Reversed Four of Wands

This cars is one of the few lesser cards, which retain its positive message despite minimal nuances.

When reversed, this card shows that you don't have the time you need to focus on doing what you love - from socializing, pursuing creative projects, or traveling. You may also experience some disruptions in your plans.

If you feel out of place, consider if your environment is fit for you. There is a chance that it is the people around you and not you.

This unsettling environment will soon pass as the positive element of this card still dominates the reading.

Three of Wands

Character: Three of Wands

Element: Fire

Astrological Sign/ Planet: Sun in Aries

General Interpretation: Adventure and action

This is the only card in the Tarot deck that features a person with no visible face.

This man is an adventurer as signified by his red and green cloak.

Like the Magician, he also wears a thin headband, which symbolizes the mind and his willpower to succeed.

The Upright Three of Wands

This card, when upright, is a card of good fortune. It reveals successful completion of your projects. It is also a positive indicator for weddings and important relationships.

The Three of Wands also predicts a busy, intense period of activity - so you should be ready to be inundated with visitors, calls, emails, and texts.

This card is also the card of nonconformism and individuality, so you may find yourself attracted to unconventional projects or people in the next few days.

The Reversed Three of Wands

If reversed, the Three of Wands reveals communication problems. Plans could be delayed and it could be challenging to make progress in your projects.

Your relationships may suffer as you may find it hard to express yourself and understand what other people are saying.

Misunderstandings may make you feel unnecessarily alone.

But take note that these are only minor irritations, as in general, this card is a card of good fortune.

Two of Wands
Character: Two of Wands

Element: Fire

Astrological Sign/ Planet: Mars in Aries

General Interpretation: Influence, partnerships, plans

The Two of Wands card portrays a young man holding a wand in his left hand and a globe in his right hand. The man is holding the wand on its base, and he rests it on an elevated section of a wall so it is taller than him.

The symbols in this card offers meaning of extension - to look beyond the immediate future. Standing at the top of a castle, this man is watching over a peaceful lake.

The man has plans, and they are starting to grow as signified by the budding leaves in the two wands.

The Upright Two of Wands

You are making forward with your plans. In the workplace, you are gaining influence and proving your worth.

In return, you can receive good advice and support. This card can also show new beginnings and creative partnerships.

The two wands in the card signify two aspects of your present situation. Carefully consider what is helping you on your path as well as any issues that are holding you back.

Your talent will continue to shine if you maximize your strength.

The Reversed Two of Wands

If reversed, your talent might be wasted because the people who are capable of helping you are not listening to you. Hence, you need to consider a change of scenery.

You should be with people who understand your views and who are appreciative of your skills.

Ace of Wands
Character: Ace of Wands

Element: Fire

Astrological Sign/ Planet: Sagittarius, Leo, Aries

General Interpretation: Beginnings, travel, career, enterprise

This card features a hand appearing from a cloud and offering one wand.

Among the cards in the suit of wands, this is the only one that shows several buds, which symbolizes new ventures.

The lower stems have three leaves, while the one stem on the top of the wan has four leaves.

But there are 18 leaves in total as there are floating leaves around the wand. Below the wand, we can see purple mountains, which is associated with spirituality.

There is also a castle on top of a hill, which signifies the dream to achieve a dream or spiritual aspiration.

The Upright Ace of Wands

This is a good fortune card for every aspect of your life. In a reading, it counters any negative minor arcana cards.

The Ace predicts invention, new beginnings, and enterprise, and often related to projects and work issues.

This is also a positive card for creative projects. The Ace of Wands will also serve as your inspiration to plan what you will do next.

The wand is also a phallic symbol, which is associated with male fertility and beginning a new family.

If two or more Aces appear near each other in a layout, it means the following:

- Two Aces – an important partnership
- Three Aces - good news
- Four Aces - beginnings, excitement

The Reversed Ace of Wands

If the Ace of Wands appears in reverse, it may signify delays to travel and blocks to creative projects.

In the workplace, a project may be postponed or even cancelled because of poor management.

Another common interpretation of this reversed card is difficulty in conceiving a child especially if the card appears with the Three of Swords or the heartbreak card.

Chapter 6. Interpreting Minor Arcana Cards: The Suit Of Swords

CARD	MEANING
King of Swords	A strong-willed man, also divorce
Queen of Swords	An independent woman
Knight of Swords	An opponent
Page of Swords	Gossip, contracts
Ten of Swords	Endings
Nine of Swords	Anxiety

Eight of Swords	Restriction
Seven of Swords	Theft
Six of Swords	Leaving conflict behind
Five of Swords	Conflict
Four of Swords	Rest
Three of Swords	Heartbreak
Two of Swords	Stalemate
Ace of Swords	Success

King of Swords
Character: King of Swords

Element: Air of the Suit of Air

Astrological Sign/ Planet: Capricorn and Aquarius

General Interpretation: An ambitious man

The King of Swords is associated with The Emperor or the symbol of father image who brings authority, order, and structure.

Mind is the domain of the King of Swords just as the King of Wands the soul, the King of Pentacles, the physical body, and the King of Cups, the heart.

The King has a regal ensemble and has similarities to the Justice. His throne is decorated with butterfly motifs, signifying the element of the Air. There is also a female fairy on his right.

The two crescents that form a crest with the butterflies at the top of his throne resemble sickles, which is another tool that cuts like a sword. In all his regality, this King is charming but can be ruthless.

The Upright King of Swords

The King of Swords can be a logical man or a male figure who depends on his intellect to win. He welcomes ideas, even though he can be impatient if he has to wait for other people before he takes action. But he is calm and make sound judgements. He is quite charming and has a dry sense of humor.

In card layouts, he can appear as a charming man you meet at work or via other business connections. His ideal vocations include conventional professions, and you will usually find him in powerful roles such as lawyer, professor, judge, or doctor. In the workplace, he is often a director or a manager.

Regardless of the profession he chooses, he must be able to make decisions that could make a difference.

If this card appears in your card reading (in an upright position) it means that you have to take charge. However, you should focus on the mind instead of the heart. You might be going through an intensive time at work.

You should also take the initiative when it comes to domestic affairs and your personal relationships.

Here are the interpretations if you get two or more Kings in your reading:

> Two Kings - a viable partnership
>
> Three Kings - circle of influence
>
> Four Kings - a battle for power

The Reversed King of Swords

If reversed, the influence of the balanced king could be damaging. You may be placed under unreasonable stress to produce results.

However, there's no room for personal interpretations or arguments, so you might feel oppressed. But because this is just a minor card, this situation is temporary.

Also, this card also suggests that you may need to deal with someone who is playing mind games and who is willing to do anything in order to win.

Queen of Swords
Character: Queen of Swords

Element: Water of the suit of Air

Astrological Sign/ Planet: Virgo and Libra

General Interpretation: An incisive woman

The Queen of Swords is associated with The Empress or the symbol of mother figure.

This royalty is the 'mind' aspect of the mother, just as the heart is the realm of the Queen of Cups.

This Queen has a sense of sovereignty like no other as she is the only royal female figure shown like a head on a coin. Her hand is raised as if she is greeting a visitor.

Similar to the Queen of Wands, she is alert, signifying that she is in charge. She also holds her swords at the right angle to her throne arm and sits on a raised ground. This provides her a sense of authority over her realm.

The Upright Queen of Swords

The Queen of Swords is traditionally known as the widow or pertains to a woman who has to make her own way in the world. This is also a common card for single parents. The Queen urges you to stand strong and push your determination as she offers her intelligence, wisdom, perspective, and ability to see the bigger picture.

If appears near a negative card in a reading, the Queen shows strength in the midst of adversity.

Remember that the interpretation may vary depending on the number of queens in your reading: two queens may mean rivalry, three means helpful friends and four may signify a gathering of women.

The Reversed Queen of Swords

When reversed, this minor arcana card suggests that you are in a situation in which you are attacked unfairly or you are making excuses for bad behavior.

You may need to deal with an opponent or an individual who has suddenly turned vengeful and bitter.

The usual reason for the Queen to invert could be extreme stress. this female royalty lacks awareness of just how unreasonable the pressure has become. If you are in this situation, you should back away.

Knight of Swords

Character: Knight of Swords

Element: Fire of the suit of Air

Astrological Sign/ Planet: Gemini and Taurus

General Interpretation: Truth and stress

The Knight of Swords is shown in full battle gear. He seems to be in the middle of a battle with his swords raised, and his feet forced down into the stirrups so his horse will keep pace.

However, his visor is raised, which shows that he is ready to look into the eyes of his enemy. He is against the wind, which is a sign that he is not afraid to ride towards opposition. The landscape is mostly barren, which is a symbol for survival. His sword reaches the edges of the card, which suggests that his intention goes beyond the limited landscape. Focused on his mission, nothing may stop this Knight.

The Upright Knight of Swords

Tempestuous and unpredictable times are ahead. You may experience a roller coaster drama. Underlying conflicts may be exposed or sudden truths may come to light. Depending on your position, you may find this bewildering, stressful, or illuminating.

This card usually comes up to show disputes at work as well as tension within families and in romantic relationships. Even though you may not be responsible for the root of the problem, what is important now is how you can rise up. You need to move forward, but you may have to wait until the situation is more peaceful before you make a move.

If you get two or more Knights in a reading, the interpretations are as follows:

> Two Knights - Righteous friendship but rivalry if one or both cards are reversed
>
> Three Knights - Meeting of men
>
> Four Knights - Events speed up, lots of action

The Reversed Knight of Swords

The reversed arrival of the King of Swords means stressful circumstances that could be blown out of proportion. It also pertains to a person who thrives on emotions but has no ability to take control of the situation.

This card also predicts that you may need to be let down by someone you thought was steadfast and reliable. An individual with a big personality may have many things to say but have minimal substance. But the person's intelligence means he has the ability to talk his way out of a situation and deny any involvement.

Page of Swords

Character: Page of Swords

Element: Earth of the suit of Air

Astrological Sign/ Planet: None

General Interpretation: Contracts and intelligence

This Minor Arcana card portrays a young man who stands strong, sword brandished using his both hands and alert to the signs of any attack.

The background is dominated by clouds, and there are few trees that are blown over by the wind.

The flock of birds suggest that something is about to take form or flight. Regardless of what may happen, the Page of Swords is ready for action during times of trouble.

His position is the best position to counter any attack. He stands tall for all to see his sword, which is a weapon of his mind and intention that similar to the Knight of Swords extend beyond the edge of this card.

The young man is open to deal with known and unknown threats to plan his response and ultimately win. Even though he is not dressed for battle - he has no armor and possible no background in warfare. His position suggests that he is ready to defend or attack.

He looks over his right shoulder away from his sword, which is a sign that he is on high alert.

The Upright Page of Swords

This card signifies valuable information. Your hard work is now paying off in business and other professional dealings. This one also suggests that people around you are supportive to realize your dreams.

However, this is also a time to be alert and carefully observe what other people are saying. Be ready to take action as you see the right opportunity and consult others who may act as advocates on your behalf.

This lesser card also appears in readings to note that a contract will be coming your way usually about travel documents, careers, or property.

The Reversed Page of Swords

If reversed, this witty Page becomes shrewd and manipulative. Be careful about the information you receive now, as it may not be reliable. Be cautious about what you hear about other people, as it may be unreliable and even untrue.

Ten of Swords

Character: Ten of Swords

Element: Air

Astrological Sign/ Planet: Mercury in Virgo

General Interpretation: Endings

This card has a black background, which can also be seen in the Devil and the Nine of Swords. This is indeed a negative card as it depicts a young man stabbed at the back by 10 swords.

There's also a sense of shock in the card, signified by the yellow sky dominated by black clouds or heavy rain.

The sky represents two worlds, which is the bright outlook of the world before the conflict, in which everything can be changed and an abrupt descends like a shroud to cover the body.

The victim is slumped and we can't see his face as if he is no longer important. This card focuses on the swords, instead. His hand is slightly twisted, and if you take a closer look, you can see it forms the blessing sign of the Hierophant.

As such, we may interpret the figure as a fallen guru or master. This position could also be a sign that the victim has already accepted his ending. He is draped by red cloth, and this fabric flows like blood from the body. Red is the color of love and life.

The Upright Ten of Swords

The conventional interpretation of this card is ruin. Even though this sounds frightening, it does not mean destruction or death.

Also take note that the scene depicted in this card, while abrupt, has a background story. This is not an act of Nature similar to the lightning strike in the Tower. This is a result of a series of events, which results in inevitable change.

This culmination clears the way for new possibilities. This ending could release you from stress and frustration. As such, this card is associated with the Death card in terms of new beginnings, transition, and endings.

In your personal relationships, you may see some break up with your close friends, and there's no going back. Sadly, this is unavoidable, but with hindsight, you can see that some people in your circle will cause stress or discord.

In romantic relationships, this card signifies a dramatic culmination, especially if it appears with the Three of Cups.

This card usually applies to a group of people, instead of individuals. In the workplace, this may manifest as the closure of a project accompanied by failing business or loss of employment.

In a more positive interpretation, this signals the end of an era. The stress and chaos will be soon over. Health issues like exhaustion and energy will also improve.

The Reversed Ten of Swords

If reversed, this card contains the essence of the upright card. However, it also signifies that there may be more repercussions.

You may recall your past actions and feel angry or guilty and react more deeply to the breakup. Avoid being affected too much by stress.

Just accept the situation and learn to let go. This card may also show feeling helpless, especially if you have been sick or overwhelmed by your emotions. You will soon recuperate and start over.

Nine of Swords

Character: Nine of Swords

Element: Air

Astrological Sign/ Planet: Mars in Gemini

General Interpretation: Anxiety

This card is another negative card. It portrays a figure in despair sitting upright in bed. It is already night, but he is awake and anguished.

Nine swords appear in the background. While swords represent thoughts and intellect, in this card, it signifies restriction.

The lowest sword seems to cut through the figure's heart while the second sword from the bottom strikes through his head that oppresses him. This figure is stressed in the mind and in the heart. He is also cut off from the obvious sources of comfort in a desperate struggle within.

The scene depicted on the bed side invokes a dreamy scene. However, the two figures portrayed are not at peace. There is an anguished tone in the decoration.

But in contrast to the negative aura of this card, the blanket is beautiful and bright. It shows the 12 signs of the zodiac with patches of red roses.

The symbols of the zodiac signifies multitude instead of any individual importance. These glyphs are trying to tell you that your worries may encompass your life.

The red roses are a symbol of hope and love. The figure cannot see hope yet because he covers his eyes.

The Upright Nine of Swords

You may have been sick for a while and the resulting low energy or a buildup of minor worries or trauma is now starting your peace of mind.

External events such as these may have triggered the initial worry, but the issue now is how you will respond to it. Look at the nearby cards to see the life area, which is relevant to your card, even though the anxiety in this card may reflect sadness in important life areas from personal relationships to the workplace.

This card also signifies the habit of anxiety, so you may be worrying about trivial things that you usually don't mind. Fortunately, as this is a lesser card, this is only temporary.

In the workplace, this card indicates that you feel overwhelmed. You basically have too much on your plate, especially if this card arrives with the Ten of Wands, which signifies burden.

The Reversed Nine of Swords

The reversed Nine of Swords reflects a more negative aura than the upright card. This card traditionally means feeling stuck, guilt, or despair.

If you get this card, bear in mind that this is the lowest point in the sequence, and soon, your anxiety will start to shift.

As you eventually move out of this challenging stage, you will feel more capable of turning your feelings of powerlessness. Learn how to wait and be kind to yourself. Share your problems with the people who really care about you. Don't carry your burdens alone.

Eight of Swords
Character: Eight of Swords

Element: Air

Astrological Sign/ Planet: Jupiter in Gemini

General Interpretation: Restriction

This card tells a story gone bad - a young female has been banished from the castle, and her hands are tied.

She is alone inside a semicircle of planted swords, with her back turned to the castle. An isolated figure, this is the archetype of disassociation. He is far away from the castle, which symbolizes inclusion and civilization.

Her red dress is a symbol of vitality, but this energy cannot be used so it is restricted. The rock pools look innocuous and pretty, but if the maiden cannot change her position soon, the rising water can be dangerous to her life. Her eyes are covered, signifying an inability to see the path ahead.

The Upright Eight of Swords

You feel trapped at the moment. This may be caused by a series of poor luck and bad experiences, and you start to wonder if things will ever improve.

You may feel anxiety because of an unsatisfactory bond with an organization or a person. Specifically, you may be trapped by a financial agreement, which leaves you with little money for yourself.

This negative card usually reveals problems in the workplace and the mental or intellectual domain, demonstrating disappointment and at its most extreme, chaos.

At present, you may find it challenging to do your work because of disorganized management or unreasonable demands.

Moreover, there may be a sense of talk going behind your back so you feel disassociated and even open to attacks.

The card also results in readings to show a person who is not fit for the role, but still working for the sake of conformity. Maybe you are forced to work in a family business or you take a course because it will lead to a high-paying career, even though it is not what you really love to do.

Many creatives go through this ordeal of conforming. However, it may take time and confidence to look for your path. You may release yourself from these restrictions, but it may take some determination, and you may have to swallow your pride and ask other people for advice and support.

On a social level, the Eight of Swords may show you feeling ignored or humiliated, and you are also worried about the attitude of other people towards you.

The Reversed Eight of Swords

Much of the upright interpretation of this card also applies in the reverse position, except that it is usually accompanied by strong emotions such as regret, anger, and guilt.

But it is likely that you express these feelings in negative ways because you are so disappointed. Avoid lashing out the people that are closest to you. As with all the lesser cards, the Eight of Swords is only temporary.

Seven of Swords

Character: Seven of Swords

Element: Air

Astrological Sign/ Planet: Moon in Aquarius

General Interpretation: Dishonesty and theft

A thief is trying to run away carrying five of seven swords from an unguarded encampment.

This appears to be an easy job as the doors of the tent are open, and their flashy colors make them enticing to anyone.

The thief is aware that he is safe with his stolen swords and even smirks as he looks back at the encampment, knowing full well he will not be caught.

The yellow background of this card signifies consciousness, so the character is not hiding his deed. This is a thief in the middle of the day.

His clothes are also flashy, and his red boots and hat gives the impression of someone with a sense of pride and taste for the finer things in life - except, he is willing to possess these things by any means necessary.

The color red also signifies the material world. The red boots suggest that the man acts on his ego to achieve his goals.

But it is curious that the thief only stole five swords. The remaining swords provides this card a positive aura. The swords can be used by the victims to protect themselves, even if the opponent has the edge.

The Upright Seven of Swords

The traditional name for this card is the Thief, and its core message is to safeguard your properties and possessions.

This card also predicts a potential challenge to your position. There may be a person who will try to invade your space, or in relationships, your partner may take too much from you or even defraud you.

Because the swords symbolizes intellect, you need your wits and instinct to uncover the truth. You may need to be scheming and take this person for a ride.

Your enemy may have the advantage, but you still have important resources by your side. This card may also predict legal problems and fraudulent or unfair business transactions.

The Reverse Seven of Swords

The reversed arrival of this card shows your tendency to quit instead of holding your ground. You may feel that you are not skilled enough to think like your enemy to anticipate their next moves.

However, this attitude can help you defend what is yours. Otherwise, you may give up too soon.

This card reflects your workplace if a colleague is trying to take power from you. It is crucial to hold your ground. As with the upright version of this card, the reversed one also predicts legal problems or shady business dealings.

Six of Swords

Character: Six of Swords

Element: Air

Astrological Sign/ Planet: Mercury in Aquarius

General Interpretation: Moving on

This card is one of the most positive cards in the Sword suit alongside the Four of Swords (Peace) and Ace of Swords (Winning).

In this card, there are stress, blindfolds, and battles. It portrays a ferryman steering a boat to a more peaceful destination with gentle trees and hills.

Take note of the calm water before the boat but the water on the right is choppy. The troubled water signifies a rough situation that the man is moving away from and the still waters ahead is a time of serenity away from chaos.

The ferryman has two passengers - a shrouded person and a child, possible a mother and child. They face away from the reader, which suggests that they are focused on their destination. They already made a decision, and the journey has started.

The Upright Six of Swords

You are moving on from a relationship or a situation and you will enjoy a time of harmony and peace. This may manifest mentally instead of physically as you are more detached in your approach. You want to stay away from complications and drama.

This provides you a chance to recharge and rest. It may cause you to make a spiritual discovery or explore a new environment. In the workplace, this card shows travel as part of your role as well as a respite from the office or other workplace.

In personal relationships, the card usually shows two people who are about to spend time apart. It may also mean an end to a relationship, especially if this card appears alongside Three of Swords (heartbreak).

In a much simpler interpretation, this card suggests taking a break from your usual environment or taking a break from work. You may also travel for a longer period if this card appears alongside The Chariot.

The Reversed Six of Swords

If reversed, the Six of Swords has a meaning, which is similar to that of its upright counterpart. It suggests a need for a temporary escape, but this plan will be delayed.

Perhaps, it is not the right time for you to travel or leave an unsatisfying situation as specific problems should be resolved or addressed before you can be free.

But check if your intentions are sound and that you are searching for the right direction, instead of focusing on a specific result. You may feel disappointed no by lack of progress, but keep your focus and grounded.

Five of Swords
Character: Five of Swords

Element: Air

Astrological Sign/ Planet: Venus in Aquarius

General Interpretation: Conflict, loss, upheaval

This card depicts a young man holding three swords, one downward and two hoisted at his shoulder.

Two swords are lying down on the beach, possibly used by the retreating men. Instead of having dignity in victory, the man appears to be smirking, possibly feeling pleasure in the defeat of his enemies.

The retreating figures have their backs against the reader suggesting that they are not able to face the challenger. The figure on the right covers his face in shame.

The clouds reflect the story of the conflict, which has just ended. They are slashed and gray similar to torn fabric. The youth wears green (the color of nature) and red (energy and vitality).

This also tells us about the personality of the man. Red reflects his ego and energy and green suggests his sense of natural entitlement. He enjoys his enemy's humiliation.

The Upright Five of Swords

The conventional interpretation of this Minor Arcana card is loss in battle. It usually predicts conflicts at the workplace or at home and also being under the scrutiny of the system such as authorities.

In personal relationships, this card predicts conflict and tension. In general, this card reveals continuous challenges to your position, ongoing stress, and mostly defeat.

But all is not lost. You may not win this round, but you can still rise up and walk away with your dignity as long as you make a gracious exit at the right time.

There's a risk here that you still fight even if the battle is over. Manage your anger and frustration regardless of the provocation.

The Reversed Five of Swords

The reversed Five of Swords predict unnecessary tension. You may become trapped in the middle of other people's fight and you may receive the most injury.

This battle is not for good reason. The person who started the battle has his own self-interest in mind and he may be trying to cover up his or her faults so there is a need to demonstrate his power.

As such, it may be easier for you to extricate yourself because you know that this battle is not personal. Another interpretation of this card is oppression and bullying. There's no shame in this. Instead, the card suggests looking for an opportunity to expose the inequality and to change the balance of power.

Four of Swords

Character: Four of Swords

Element: Air

Astrological Sign/ Planet: Jupiter in Libra

General Interpretation: Quiet time, passivity, rest

Placed between the Three of Swords (Heartbreak) and the Five of Swords (Battle), this card offers rest or the opportunity to rise up from the onslaught of the Five and the betrayal and stress of the Three.

The knight portrayed in this card has temporarily laid down his tools. A sword is shown lengthwise with the hilt aligned with the man's head.

The other three swords are hanging above the knight, fastened in the wall, ready for the knight when he wakes up. But at this point, the knight is resting, safe from attack as well as the demands of tension.

The stained-glass window signifies that the world is being held at a distance during the man's quiet time. The stained-glass depicts a monk assisting a child, which reflects the commitment of a medieval knight to charity. This is reflected in the code of chivalry.

The Upright Four of Swords

The traditional interpretation of this card is time out. You are taking a rest from a relationship, personal project or from work. This card usually comes up in card layouts in the past or present to show taking a break from a relationship and also the need for recuperation.

This card also suggests recovery from stress, so you may need to preserve your energy and take rest as much as you can. The isolation of the figure in this card also applies to lightworkers and mediators as well as other people who follow a spiritual path.

You may need more private time and mental space than the usual, so in this sense, the card is a nudge to take some time alone for recovery.

The Reversed Four of Swords

The reversed arrival of this card enforces the need for rest. So you have to take a break from work or other obligations. You cannot avoid this need for a break as this will be caused by powers way beyond your control.

Sadly, there is little you can do to change this situation. Hence, you should surrender to events. Use the rest time positively. You may have to rethink your work situation or come to terms with sudden shift in your relationships, especially if you are now living apart from your partner or potential love.

Three of Swords

Character: Three of Swords

Element: Air

Astrological Sign/ Planet: Saturn in Libra

General Interpretation: Pain, heartbreak, sorrow

This card portrays an enlarged heart stabbed by three swords. The background is also bleak with clouds and rain, which enforces the action of the swords. They are like arrows stabbing the gray sky.

But surprisingly, this card has the subtle blue sheen on the lower part of the swords, which suggest truth.

The swords pierce through the truth. Possibly, after all the chaos, a clear sky is waiting for brighter days ahead.

This is one of the two lesser cards that don't portray human figures (the other is the VIII of Wands. Hence, there's no clear action for interpretation.

This is by design, because the primary focus is the effect of the swords, giving the cards its primary meaning of heartbreak.

Swords basically symbolizes the mind, but in this card, we are dealing with emotional pain (a realm of emotions). The swords lend drama to the situation. However, the pain is very much in the heart instead of the head.

The Upright Three of Swords

This card shows the pain of truth, and there's nothing you can do but face the reality. This is a traditional card for betrayal in relationships and may signify disloyalty or affairs.

In a more positive interpretation, you are capable of going right to the heart of the matter. You can easily banish any confusion, and you are now in a position to start to move on from the trauma. You will soon start the healing process and move on.

The Reversed Three of Swords

The upright interpretation of this card comes with drama and conflict. In a sense, despite the chaos, this will provide you with a more positive interpretation compared to the upright version of this card. The people around you will understand your need to vent out your emotions.

Two of Swords

Character: Two of Swords

Element: Air

Astrological Sign/ Planet: Moon in Libra

General Interpretation: Stalemate, time to think

An isolated and blindfolded maiden is holding two swords across her chest. It seems that she is taking a break from a duel and she is guarding her heart with the swords.

She appears to be afraid that the heartbreak of the Three of Swords will attack her.

Even though blindfolded similar to the lady in the Eight of Swords, the maiden portrayed in this card is in a safer place. Sitting on an elevated ground, this is her place for thinking.

Her bluish clothes is in monastic theme that signifies the lady is taking a break from the material world and keeping her thoughts in the meantime.

The partially submerged rocks signifies issues that are about to surface in the next few days. The maiden's hair is parted in a way that her third eye can be seen.

While she can't see using her physical eyes, she has the intuitive visual prowess. The twilight sky mirrors a shift in the emotional self.

The lady is contemplating about two major options, which is also noted by the appearance of the two swords.

The Upright Two of Swords

You need to take your time before making a decision. The situation is now a stalemate, so you can take this time as a rest before you resume negotiation.

Your tendency at this point is to guard yourself, have a bit of peace, and don't take action at the moment.

Sadly, this upcoming battle may not go away. You have to handle it now so you can be done with it. Or else, the situation will just fester and will return.

The two swords predict that you have to deal with a person you are crossing swords with. This person may have a sharp tongue. But hold your ground and don't give in to the lashing. You should say what is on your mind.

This card usually appears in readings to show workplace issues as well as the need to take a break from your personal relationships.

If this card appears with the Reversed Loves or the Three of Swords, it signifies making a decision about the future of your relationship.

The Reversed Two of Swords

If reversed, the conventional meaning of the Two of Swords is deception and being blind to the manipulation of a person close to you.

This card is specifically applicable to partnerships - business, friendships or love. If your gut is telling you that someone is not being honest, listen and perform your own investigation so you can get to the bottom of the issue.

Do not delay taking action because the timing here is sensitive.

Ace of Swords
Character: Ace of Swords
Element: Air

Astrological Sign/ Planet: Aquarius, Libra, and Gemini

General Interpretation: Beginnings, decisions, success

A magical cloud produces a hand holding an upright sword. Added with a crown, this image is the symbol of the Kether or the Tree of Life.

The crown also hangs a sprig of mistletoe and frond of fern. As these plants are capable of attaching themselves to trees, the sword has become a symbol of strength.

Near the hilt of the sword are six golden leaves, which reminds us of the leaves in the Ace of Wands. This number is associated with Zain or the 6th letter of the Hebrew alphabet.

The number 6 is also associated with the Lovers, which signify decisions as any action or inaction with the sword is decisive. The landscape under the sword portrays purple and blue mountains, which signify goals and spiritual truth.

Even though there are no green pastures or dwellings, growth is reflected on the crown. The fern and mistletoe signify the fertility of the mind. Therefore, the sword provides us the gift of intelligence (associating with the Air element of the card, for the realm of the mind).

Similar with other Ace cards, this card is offered using the right hand or the giving hand as opposed to the left hand or the hand of receiving.

The Upright Ace of Swords

The Ace of Swords is considered auspicious. In a reading, it dominates any negative lesser cards nearby. Its effect is similar to the Sun. It predicts clear thinking, decisions, and new beginnings. It also relates to love and work.

This card also heralds confrontation, drama, and action. But the Ace of Swords manifests in your life and will bring an immediate change based on your circumstances.

As a divination card, it reflects the assertiveness and mental agility. The other cards nearby the Ace in a reading will point you in the direction of your conquest. However, you should be cautious.

Be direct without being abrasive. Be conscious of how you would want to be treated if you are the receiving party.

Note that getting two or more Aces in your reading could mean different things:

- Two Aces - important partnership
- Three Aces - good news
- Four Aces - beginnings, excitement, potential

The Reversed Ace of Swords

The reverse arrival of this card predicts arguments and conflicts. You may also become involved in a damaging battle of wills. It also foretells a challenge that you may not able to overcome for now.

You may need to withdraw, recuperate, and direct your focus on other important aspects of your life. You may also lack the confidence in your intellectual abilities for now and you don't feel at par with the people around you. However, this is only your perception and not the actual reality.

Another traditional interpretation of the Ace of Swords is a decision going against you such as failing at a job interview or an exam. You may also not able to stand your ground when you encounter a more dominant personality.

Chapter 7. Interpreting Minor Arcana Cards: The Suit Of Pentacles

CARD	MEANING
King of Pentacles	A prosperous man
Queen of Pentacles	A generous woman
Knight of Pentacles	A dependable man
Page of Pentacles	An offer
Ten of Pentacles	Marriage, good business, inheritance
Nine of Pentacles	Material comforts
Eight of Pentacles	Money coming
Seven of Pentacles	Potential for success
Six of Pentacles	Generosity
Five of Pentacles	Financial loss, exclusion

Four of Pentacles	Stability
Three of Pentacles	Showing your talent
Two of Pentacles	Decisions
Ace of Pentacles	Success, beginnings

King of Pentacles

Character: King of Pentacles

Element: Air of the Suit of Earth

Astrological Sign/ Planet: Taurus and Aries

General Interpretation: A generous man

The King of Pentacles is associated with The Emperor or the father symbol who brings authority, order, and structure. He also deals with practical concerns, property, and money for a more secure life.

The head of a boar on his left foot represents his control on base instincts . The King's foot and leg are armored which stands for the hard labor to achieve his position. Showing supremacy, his crown is decorated with red flowers and fleur de lis that are symbols for fertility from ancient Egyptians.

The images of bulls and grapes in the picture are similar with the ancient legend of Ampelos, a young satyr loved by the Greek god of wine named Dionysus.

When Ampelos was killed by a feral bull, Dionysus turned his blood into wine and his body into grapevine. The red grapes and vines spreads around the King's robes and the bull's head that signifies success and fruitfulness. This only means that the King plans thoroughly and anticipates outcome from long-term investments.

He rests a large-golden coin on his left knee with his left hand while holding a scepter with his right. He is stationed inside the castle battlements that is protected by a stone wall.

Castle towers and keep are prominent on the right side of the card making the King protected and secured. With the orange and golden background similar to his coin, the warm sky tells us it's the season of harvest - a symbol of abundance. The King does not rest on his laurels for his red cowl means the energy and the physical world.

The Upright King of Pentacles

As a person, the King of Pentacles refers to a visionary man who has a plan. He is driven to work hard to achieve his goals and he is usually wealthy. He is also supportive, generous, and reliable. Security is also important for him. He yearns for a more stable relationship.

He needs to be a protector because of his firm boundaries. He has zero tolerance for those who are trying to take what is his. His ideal professions include business, property, finance or any work that relies on numbers or land management.

If two or more Kings appear in a reading, the interpretations are as follows:

- Two Kings - A good partnership
- Three Kings - Men of influence
- Four Kings - Power struggle

The Reversed King of Pentacles

If reversed, the King of Pentacles is untrustworthy and greedy. Therefore, you must carefully check all financial dealings to make sure that there are no unfair caveat.

This card could also mean debt, so focus well on your finances to limit the effects of overspending.

The King refers to a corrupt person who may be involved in gambling or fraud. He has the drive to win at any cost.

Queen of Pentacles

Character: Queen of Pentacles

Element: Water of the Suit of Earth

Astrological Sign/ Planet: Capricorn and Sagittarius

General Interpretation: A reliable woman

The Queen of Pentacles is associated with the Empress or the symbol of motherhood. She also represents the material or physical side of the mother, so she deals with practical concerns, property, and money.

This royal figure looks down on her golden coin as well as to the Earth as her suit of element. Surrounding her are symbols of fertility and spring - the flowers, the flowing water, lush vegetation, and the hare.

The rose briar is also portrayed in the Magician and the Strength card that also shares the dominant colors of yellow and red for clear sightedness and practicality.

The landscape is partly wild and cultivated, giving the sense that work is continuing and that the Queen is quite comfortable in nature and in the domain of her yard or garden. She cares for her environment, pragmatic, and most importantly, she knows how to work to achieve her goals.

She has the patience and will wait to see her rewards. Her throne portrays pears, which are symbols of long life and fertility. This fruit is also sacred to the ancient Roman deity Pomona.

The Queen's crown also features a winged goat as a reflection of Capricorn, which is one of the Queen's zodiacs. The goal also appears on the Devil card signifying excess, and in the case of the Queen of Pentacles, this translates to sensuality.

The Upright Queen of Pentacles

As a person, the Queen of Pentacles is often supportive, generous, and well off. She is wise, affectionate, and has a strong maternal instinct. She represents a woman who has wisdom beyond her years.

Her professions include entrepreneurship, sport coaching, politics, agriculture, ecology, public office - or any career that is driven by dealing with a lot of people. She is also an ideal housewife as she loves taking care of her home or garden.

This Queen loves the good things in life and knows how to spend money well - on beautiful things, on presents for loved ones, and also on herself. She is hands-on in her projects and physically affectionate. Instead of dictating from the sidelines, she is active in offering her helping hand. She usually shows up in readings as a benefactor.

The main message of this card is to take care of your body as well as your finances. Aside from financial help, money management, wisdom and support, the Queen of Pentacles predicts marriage or money from a generous couple. It is also an auspicious card for children, fertility, sensual sex life, and good health.

The Reversed Queen of Pentacles

Your finances may suffer if you see this card on reverse. The money you are expecting will not roll in or will not be properly spent. You may need to deal with the effect of someone's financial challenges. But this is just temporary.

An additional interpretation is you might be ignoring your domestic affairs while you are too busy with your other concerns.

As a person, the reversed Queen can be unimaginative and stubborn. She may spend big sums based on emotions and she can be mean with money. Her erratic behavior is for self-comfort or she uses financial leverage to win over the affection of the people around her.

Knight of Pentacles
Character: Knight of Pentacles

Element: Fire of the Suit of Earth

Astrological Sign/ Planet: Virgo and Leo

General Interpretation: Improving prosperity

This is an interesting card as this is the only Knight in the four minor suits of the Tarot whose horse is not galloping.

The Knight's steed is made for pulling a plough instead of raging into battle. This signifies a measured approach, which is quite unlike the Knight of Swords who rushes headlong towards his mission.

The Knight of Pentacles is long-term. He has no interest in fast-paced action and will work long and hard to ensure his victory.

The Knight's helmet and the plumes on the horse bridle are green, which is the color of nature. They look like a bunch of oak leaves, which reminds us of a saying "from acorns great oaks come."

This provides us the interpretation of future investment, which is a message supported by a land of rich terracotta soil. This is the right time for planting, and you can even visualize the Knight sowing his golden coin in the land and waiting for money to grow.

The Knight of Pentacles is strategic, logical, and has the ability to think several steps ahead. He is prepared for his mission. The cover under the saddle shows that he has equipped his horse for a long ride. We can also see a book, which he probably brought along to read when he stops for a break or maybe it is a notebook in which he can record his progress.

The element of this card is Fire in the suit of Earth. As such, this Knight has all the important ingredients for a stable purpose. The energy of fire drives him forward while the energy of the Earth supports him and rationalize the ideas.

The Knight's right hand holds a coin that shares the same color as the sky. Similar to the Page of Pentacles, this knight sees potential prosperity all around him. He displays his coin, which signifies that financial stability is his main concern.

His red tunic shows he has the energy, and similar to the other Tarot Knights, the color of his armor shows his true purpose.

The Upright Knight of Pentacles

As a card of good investment and financial growth, the upright arrival of this card into your reading predicts growth in your property business. You have a high chance to succeed if you strategize and set a realistic goal. Focus your attention to the practical details today, so you can ensure future benefits.

This Knight follows a steady pace, which signifies that you need to work on boring yet important tasks. In the workplace, this card may indicate more money coming to you because of a promotion, a special bonus, or a raise. However, you may have to work harder.

Another meaning of the card is looking for a secure home, probably with a partner.

The Reversed Knight of Pentacles

If reversed, the Knight of Pentacles urges you to stay away from being complacent and double check all your financial agreements. The uncomfortable meaning of this card is misleading financial advice or financial mismanagement.

Page of Pentacles
Character: Page of Pentacles

Element: Earth of the Suit of Earth

Astrological Sign/ Planet: None

General Interpretation: Finance news and talents noticed

Not similar to the Page of Swords, the Page of Pentacles is absolutely absorbed in his coin instead of the landscape around him.

He holds the coin lightly - like a precious gem - a present that will become an accolade or an award for his talents.

Around him are trees, grass, ploughed fields, and low mountains - clearly a landscape of abundance. The verdant trees nearby tells that that the Page's good fortune has come from the seeds that he tended. He admires money with the knowledge that he has its support.

Turning his focus to one issue doesn't mean any other life aspect will be neglected. There is no need for him to look over his shoulder for challengers who want a share of his wealth. As such, the Page is a symbol of wealth consciousness. He believes that he has everything that he needs with his energy and optimism.

His red headgear stands for passion and energy. He also wears a scarf that drapes over his shoulder and extending down his back, which signifies wholehearted motivation. The yellow coin and background symbolizes solar consciousness and intelligence. The Page years to show his talents.

The Page's elemental association is double Earth. What he achieves come from the ground up similar to the trees with solid roots. He starts with a sound plan and a target to build something great. As Earth of Earth, he is more practical than idealistic. He sees through his ideas, and he is steadfast to his mission.

The Upright Page of Pentacles

This card reveals adventure, progress, and fortunate beginnings. This is a good time to nurture your abilities and skills. You may receive good news about travel, education, business, or finances.

Also, this card highlights your need for organization, and in the workplace, there will be an opportunity to manage people and important projects. This Page usually appears to predict a job offer or an offer made on a real estate.

However, this card comes with a warning. You have to pay attention to details. You need to double check all agreements and arrangements. Be sure to check through all your work and personal schedule to make certain that you are still realistic about your commitments.

This card also appears if there's a need to check your finances. Pay your taxes or renew your lapsed insurance policies.

Here are the meanings if two or more Pages appear in your reading:

- Two Pages - good friendship but rivalry if one or either of the card is reversed
- Three Pages - your days will be filled with social activities
- Four Pages - you will join a social group of young individuals

The Reversed Page of Pentacles

There may be unwelcome news concerning property or finances.

Not similar to its upright and responsible counterpart, the reversed card means irresponsibility and extravagance. It also predicts suffering caused by the selfish actions of other people.

This is usually applicable to young people who are associated with immature friends. It also applies to an individual with a great sense of entitlement who doesn't mind taking what is yours.

Ten of Pentacles
Character: Ten of Pentacles

Element: Earth

Astrological Sign/ Planet: Mercury in Virgo

General Interpretation: Inheritance, family, property

This card portrays a happy couple and their child and dog. They are under the archway, which is the entrance to a wealthy home.

We can also see a house in a prosperous courtyard, and there's also a high tower that is a symbol of love, protection, learning, or tradition.

Another figure in this card is an older man who is seated in a chair resembling a throne. He is probably the King of Pentacles who is already old but still wears his cloak. He appears to bestow the couple his blessing, signifying that it is now their turn to continue the family legacy through marriage.

The card depicts three generations - the king as the grandfather, the couple, and a small child. Each generation seems separate from each other but they share the same happiness.

The position of the ten pentacles is not random. Instead, it follows the symmetry of the Tree of Life. Also, the four elements are represented equally. These elements suggest balance and harmony.

The Upright Ten of Pentacles

This card shows love relationship, generosity, and inheritance that brings happiness and wealth. So if your current concern is stability in your present relationship, the appearance of this card is good news.

This card usually comes up in a reading to predict a wedding. The couple also shares similar values and usually has similar social and cultural backgrounds.

Another interpretation is inherited property. You may soon buy a second home or extending your present home to make room for a growing family. At this point, you will also take advantage of sharing your money, skills, resources, or time to help each other out.

Take note that in this context, family may signify people whom you consider as family. Hence, this may also related to your closest friends.

The Ten of Pentacles also suggest maturity. You may see this in emotional maturity that comes with your experiences in life, as well as financial maturity when your investment grows.

The Reversed Ten of Pentacles

The reversed appearance of Ten of Pentacles show communication problems in families. One generation might be trying to dominate another. Parents and children often argue and hold different values.

This card may also highlight problems related to money or property that could test the relationships within the family. In general, attitudes toward money could be at the center of the problem. This card usually appears in readings to show overly strict older generations who are trying to control the family using money.

Nine of Pentacles
Character: Nine of Pentacles

Element: Earth

Astrological Sign/ Planet: Venus in Virgo

General Interpretation: Prosperity, accomplishment, comfort

This card depicts a prosperous woman standing proudly in her vineyard. In this land of abundance, the lady of the manor is tending not only to her grapes but also to the nine pentacles lying beside her.

These treasures are reminiscent of hay bales that are harvested and piled during the summer, with their circular ends stores like the faces of the coins.

It is interesting to note that the pentacles are not equally distributed. On her right, she has six coins, and three are on the left. The coins on the right are her prized possessions, while the coins on the left are for distribution. She ensures the sustainability of her lifestyle by ensuring that she is giving away less than what she has.

Red is the color of her hat as well as the lining of her gown. This color signifies energy and passion. It also offers a link with the womb and its significance to fertility. The flower design on her robe is associated with the glyph of Venus or the ruling planet of this card.

The bird resting on the lady's gauntlet is covered with a red hood. This shows temporary control. While birds are usually symbols of spirit, when restrained or domesticated, they also signify vanity. As the bird is not caged or chained but wears a hood, we sense that this lady is aware of the dangers of using money to gain control. She is alert against egotism and materialism.

The Upright Nine of Pentacles

The Nine predicts a time of financial stability. You will be proud of your accomplishments and you will feel safe in your home. Finally, you will be surrounded yourself with the fine things you love. You may soon find yourself redesigning your home or tend to your yard or garden.

This is also the time to appreciate all that you have. Reward yourself with whatever that makes you happy and take pleasure in the fruits of your labor. Take care of your own needs without needs minus the guilt. This card also brings you peace of mind.

In the workplace, this card predicts monetary rewards such as bonus or perks in recognition of your efforts.

The Reversed Nine of Pentacles

If reversed, this card shows egotism and vanity. Your urge for material wealth may get out of control. You need to confront overspending not only you but also your loved ones.

This card also shows financial dependence that brings discomfort or misuse of wealth for selfish ends.

An added interpretation is feeling that your domestic harmony is threatened because you are struggling with debt. There is no need to struggle alone. You can ask for support.

Eight of Pentacles

Character: Eight of Pentacles

Element: Earth

Astrological Sign/ Planet: Sun in Virgo

General Interpretation: Achievement, education

The Eight of Pentacles portray a young apprentice at work. He is quite productive, and the wood in the card - assumed as a bark of a tree that symbolizes sturdy growth - showcases his work.

The apprentice works hard, and has eight pentacles as proof. Wearing red and blue, for truth of purpose and energy, he also wears a brown apron or the traditional vestment of a smith or a mason.

Even though the apron provides the young apprentice with protection during his work, its dark color signifies protection similar to the dark cloak that you will see in the Four of Pentacles.

The budding knowledge of the apprentice will provide him financial security in the future. A solid skill and education will provide him the opportunity to live a good life.

Even though his workplace has an uncertain atmosphere (signified by the white-gray sky) he keeps his head down and he focuses on his task. The civilization can be seen in the background, so he may have made a conscious decision to work or study away from comfortable environments.

His choice to work far away from home demonstrates his ambition and commitment to walk his own path. His work is repetitive, but he does his job for mastery. He is proud of his work but he can be overly perfectionist, as one coin is lying on the floor, while others are showcased. He set his standards high and needs to uphold excellence.

The Upright Eight of Pentacles

You will soon receive a compensation, which is money that results from your previous decisions or efforts. There's a chance that you will be provided with an opportunity to master new skills that will help you to become profitable in the future.

You may also consider a new work direction or working hard for a promised promotion. Generally this card also highlights the need for a diligent and logical strategy for your projects.

This card usually shows up in a reading to predict gaining qualification or education, specifically a diploma or undergraduate degree.

The Reversed Eight of Pentacles

Do you feel trapped at the moment? This may be caused by your decision to choose educational tracks that are really not for you or you have little interest with.

At work, you may be aware that you are only doing your job for the money. Even though this may be acceptable for short-term, it may do you harm or stifle your growth.

While you are supporting your financial needs, it may be the best time to look elsewhere instead of tolerating the situation.

The Eight of Pentacles card is also a prediction tool to show that a cycle is about to come, so instead of waiting for this to happen, preserve your energy and point it towards finding a new career.

Seven of Pentacles
Character: Seven of Pentacles

Element: Earth

Astrological Sign/ Planet: Saturn in Taurus

General Interpretation: Work, potential for success

This card is also known as the card of potential success. It portrays a young man looking down at his treasure - the six pentacles on a vine and one at his feet.

The vine is reminiscent of the vine in the King of Pentacles, Nine of Pentacles and Four of Pentacles.

But in this card, the vine is established with healthy, large leaves. But notice that there are no grapes yet because the vine is not mature enough.

The young man leans on his hoe as he tends to the vine. But with effort, he will soon see the fruits of his labor.

The six pentacles on the vine show what should be set aside for the future, while the one coin symbolizes the ideal disposable income, or what you can spend now. This is a small reward today, but with patience and effort, more will come.

The young man wears blue to symbolize energy and red showing his energy. His feet, like his vine, are strongly grounded in the soil. He is probably taking stock of his accomplishment as he looks at his coins, but he needs to keep going to realize his dreams.

The Upright Seven of Pentacles

You are close in achieving your goals. However, now is not the time to stop and reflect. The Seven of Pentacles is not about philosophizing but rather it is a card of doing. Keep your focus on what you really want and believe you can accomplish it.

It may seem that you are exerting a lot of effort, but your hard work will soon pay off. This card usually appears in readings to show the need to focus on your career goals or to persist in a particularly tedious phase in a present project that is leaving you drained.

This card may also mean that your finances are not enough for the little luxuries. But regardless of your situation, just keep on, and your future self will thank you for your hard work and perseverance.

The Reversed Seven of Pentacles

If reversed, the Seven of Pentacles shows that you might be procrastinating. You might be out of time, so you need to fully commit to the work that you are doing regardless of the highs and lows.

You may also need to place your energies elsewhere. You may need to consider a different career path. You may feel disheartened with slow or zero progress in your career or your finances are currently in disarray. However, opportunities may slip away while you're in the doldrums.

Take your action now. Any decision is a lot better than no decision at all. Another interpretation of the card is depression brought by a loan or other financial agreement. If this is affecting your health, try to renegotiate the terms instead of giving up now.

Six of Pentacles
Character: Six of Pentacles

Element: Earth

Astrological Sign/ Planet: Moon in Taurus

General Interpretation: Inheritance, family, property

Similar to the figure in the Justice card (XI), the nobleman in this Minor Arcana card is holding a pair of scales, and the color of his dress is red that symbolizes practicality and energy.

Purple is the color of his mantle or the color of spirituality and intuition. This is a sign that his actions are in good faith. His tunic has blue and white stripes which is a symbol of generosity.

The young nobleman gives out coins using his right hand and his left hand weighs down the situation using the scales of mercy. There are two beggars in the card. One has a wound and wears a bandage around his head. The other beggar wears a tattered blue cloak, signifying that he is experiencing true poverty and really requires help.

The beggars are in a barren place beyond the walled city. The white-gray sky gives an uncertain feeling. It is not blue for clarity or yellow for joy. Regardless, the man still gives money.

The Upright Six of Pentacles

Money is coming to you in the form of a gift or a grant and will come from a person instead of an organization. This will allow you to settle any outstanding debt or invest it for your future.

If you have financial struggles, this card is a positive sign that your situation will really improve. Also, this card shows that you are also a generous man and will be in a position to help someone in need or you feel drawn to help a charity.

In general, this card brings authentic support and predicts you feeling connected and close to your usual circle of family and friends. An additional interpretation is receiving money or help from an individual from the past or unlocking your savings to help another person.

The Reversed Six of Pentacles

If reversed, the Six of Pentacles shows money coming to you but you will not be able to keep it. The traditional interpretation of this card is having your wallet stolen, and this message is strongly reinforced if this arrives with the Seven of Swords.

Pay attention to your possessions and keep track of your expenses so that you will have enough money in your wallet. Some people may be jealous of your money, so monitor your behavior as well as the behavior of people around you.

Another meaning is an offer of money, but it may come with conditions that are not fair to you. This card urges you not to compromise and say no if you need to. There are more options for you.

Five of Pentacles

Character: Five of Pentacles

Element: Earth

Astrological Sign/ Planet: Mercury in Taurus

General Interpretation: A test of resources

This card depicts a snowy scene with two clearly poor people suffering a harsh winter.

The man on crutches wears a bell, which in medieval times was a requirement for lepers to warn others of their approach. This signifies that the man has become untouchable and ostracized from society.

The gray-haired woman is barefoot and wears a red cloak, signifying of his persistence despite their situation. However she cannot yet understand any possibility of change.

The two impoverished figures in this card are focused on surviving the winter and they are not aware of the window near them, with its portrayal of a money tree of five pentacles and a solid, warm edifice behind it.

The stained glass window is reminiscent of church windows. As the paupers are not members of the church, and they cannot enter inside, there's a sense of exclusion from a spiritual community.

The Upright Five of Pentacles

The traditional interpretation of this card is financial loss. So when this one shows up in your reading, it may signify losing a job or you may experience some financial hardships.

On a positive note, you will find support from others in a similar position. These people will become good friends whom you may never have encountered in usual circumstances. Consider new alternatives, and you may discover another approach or resource that can help you move forward.

But this card usually comes up in readings to signify a fear of isolation and poverty instead of actual poverty. It also shows a fear of losing the security of home as an effect of a divorce or break away with one partner feeling drained and alone.

While the Tarot cards cannot predict physical demise, this card may reflect your current emotions of sadness caused by losing a loved one.

The Reversed Five of Pentacles

You need to examine your values. Are you perhaps holding on too much to something that you end up getting stuck? It's important to think about this because fear of change could be harmful. It may lead you to neglect debt or even cause you to outright ignore (if not become unintentionally oblivious) to the arising problems in your personal relationships.

Clinging to old memories and possessions show you need to feel safe for now, and you don't have the faith or confidence that you will gain support in the future. But like other Minor Arcana cards, this is just a temporary influence.

In relationships, you may suffer due to a partner's selfish behavior. Thisperson doesn't want to give to you emotionally, or he or she withholds money. The card can also show you being ill-treated by an ex-partner who doesn't pay what is due.

Four of Pentacles
Character: Four of Pentacles

Element: Earth

Astrological Sign/ Planet: Sun in Capricorn

General Interpretation: Holding on to money, self-improvement, security

The figure portrayed in the Four of Pentacles has declared himself as a king complete with a stone throne and a crown.

His goal is to elevate himself financially and socially and establish a solid base for his future.

His red gown shows that he is focused on setting up a stable foundation for himself, and now that he has accomplished this, he added a black cloak of protection to guard his possessions.

He needs to keep his possessions for himself. The components of the card are quite in harmony, which is often expressed in the number four as a symbol of balance.

But what is interesting is how connected this figure to his money. He steps on two pentacles, he holds tight to one coin against his body, and the other is attached to his crown.

Symbolically, his wealth grounds him, but also at the core of his heart and mind. His arms are wrapped around the coin to make sure no one can touch it. Wearing a coin on his crown signifies that he is proud to demonstrate that he is now a person of means and has risen through the social ladder.

The Upright Four of Pentacles

This card shows the need for stability and setting up a solid foundation. If you have experienced past hardship, this card shows the difficult times are over, as your work is now paying off. Even though this doesn't predict a significant windfall (unlike the Ten of Pentacles), your financial resources will be enough and you will also receive recognitions.

The Four of Pentacles also show protection of properties and conventional values. Establishing a solid foundation for a growing family may be crucial to you now, so you have to consider moving to a new home or investing in a business that will bring money.

In the workplace, you have achieved a position that is quite secure, so if you are working in a temporary role, this card predicts you will be offered a permanent job.

The Reversed Four of Pentacles

If reversed, this card shows an overly materialistic person who holds too fast to possessions and status. If this pertains to you, you should let go of insecurity as this may take up much of your mind. You will have an insatiable belief that you will never have enough.

In your career, this card reveals that you miss some opportunities because of low confidence, and changes to your role may leave you feeling disempowered.

As such, you need to do well in your profession and you have to put in more effort than you usually provide.

Three of Pentacles

Character: Three of Pentacles

Element: Earth

Astrological Sign/ Planet: Mars in Capricorn

General Interpretation: Success in enterprise

This card depicts a stonemason working on a church. A man wearing a strange orange cloak holds a plan. Symbolizing a lifelong commitment, a monk is also in the card, observing the work on the building.

The young mason is standing on a workbench, similar to the one used by the man portrayed in the Eight of Pentacles. The two cards both show a craftsman at work.

The three of pentacles are a part of the church's design. The young man's ideas are now part of the building structure. His contributions are now lasting and set in stone. He is working by a half-open door, which signifies that his reputation and good work will open doors for him in the future.

Purple is the color of his tunic. This is the color of high office in the church, and this shows that he is spiritually attuned with his beliefs and talents. He completely comprehends his work and knows how to direct his skills to the best effect.

It is also interesting to note that the mason appears in public, where he can be seen by people. This signifies that he is proud to demonstrate his work, and what he builds is accessible, because he believes that it is more important than the money he will receive.

This is also the card in the Pentacles suit that shows the coins in black. They represent a lasting satisfaction instead of a reward of literal golden coins.

The Upright Three of Pentacles

The upright interpretation of the Three of Pentacles is rewarding work. It usually shows that you are ready to show your talents to the public, and this card usually appears in readings for launching an enterprise or important project.

The card also predicts improvement work in your home or selling a property. It is also a good card for creative people, predicting that projects will be completed and appreciated. The work can also be shown in a public space.

The Reversed Three of Pentacles

Work is tiresome and you may not have the motivation to work at all. This may be caused by routine tasks and you doubt about success in your current career.

You need to go through the monotonous details or make a fast decision to move on. Another meaning of the card is poor planning so a project may not succeed.

Two of Pentacles

Character: Two of Pentacles

Element: Earth

Astrological Sign/ Planet: Jupiter in Capricorn

General Interpretation: Negotiation

This card portrays a young man who appears to be dancing and holding two pentacles joined by a green thread in the shape of infinity.

The same symbol appears in the Strength and the Magician cards and signifies renewal, activity, and balance.

The flow of this continuous symbol also suggests patience and consistency. For this card, the young man's concern is cash flow. It may seem that he is dancing, but he is actually juggling his coins to the tune of changing circumstances. This reinforced by the two boats in the background, which rise and fall on the waves.

The man is considering two options. He should be practical and use reason before making a decision and find harmony that is symbolized by his tall red hat. At present, his worries are in his mind and he has yet to take action.

The Upright Two of Pentacles

This card shows making a decision that mainly concerns financial management. There are temporary cash-flow concerns, and you need consistent effort in balancing the books.

If your income rises and falls, an unexpected expenses may hit you hard. This is a typical card for freelancers whose income varies. You need to pay more attention to your financial concerns so you can manage them well.

The Reversed Two of Pentacles

Pride and egotism may get in the way of practicality. Too much spending may cause problems, and these financial blunders may be hidden. Gambling is a typical reflection here as well as reckless attitude toward money.

In the workplace, you may need to deal with an unreasonable superior who is not realistic on what can be accomplished, placing you under needless pressure.

This card may also show the ending of a business partnership caused by financial hardships. One partner may be investing more resources in the business than the other. This card urges you to evaluate how dedicated you and your partners are and if the contribution is equal and fair.

Ace of Pentacles
Character: Ace of Pentacles

Element: Earth

Astrological Sign/ Planet: Capricorn, Virgo, Taurus

General Interpretation: Beginnings, property, prosperity

A heavenly cloud produces a hand that holds a big, golden coin. This is the only card in the suit of Pentacles that shows a coin with double border, as if to emphasize its value.

The landscape below the hand and the coin depicts a rose garden and cultivated lilies with an arch forming an oval archway where you can see a mountain.

This is a rich land where the owners can grow their own lilies, which is a symbol of innocence and purity. The view beyond the garden signifies challenge and the yearning for success without any obstacles.

You are offered with this wealth. The rich landscape is just an example of a luxurious lifestyle that the gift of this card may bring. The golden coin is designed with a pentagram, which is an ancient symbol for the four elements plus the fifth element or the mystical element of ether.

The Upright Ace of Pentacles

The upright interpretation of the Ace of Pentacles is good fortune in every aspect of life. In a reading, it dominates other lesser card meanings nearby similar to the effect of The Sun.

This card predicts contentment and happiness. You can have what you really desire. It also predicts prosperity and you find money comes to you easily.

As such, the card offers an opportunity for further achievement, so now is the best time to receive the gift and use it to further boost your earning potential.

Again, remember that multiple aces could mean different things: two means an important partnership, three may indicate welcome news, and four may mean new beginnings.

The Reversed Ace of Pentacles

There is greed and holding fast to one result. This desperation may cause materialistic thinking, and if you are focused on one outcome, you may ignore other important aspects of your life.

This card also reveals unwise investment of money or time, so be aware of the motives of those you invest with or work for. This can be a challenging time if you are unfairly treated by an unscrupulous individual or organization.

As a prediction card in a reading, it cautions you to delay any major financial decisions.

Chapter 8. Interpreting Minor Arcana Cards: The Suit Of Cups

CARD	MEANING
King of Cups	A warm hearted man
Queen of Cups	An intuitive woman
Knight of Cups	A proposal
Page of Cups	Socializing and fun
Ten of Cups	Family and happiness
Nine of Cups	A wish come true
Eight of Cups	Departure
Seven of Cups	Possibilities, confusion
Six of Cups	A visitor, peace
Five of Cups	Loss, sadness
Four of Cups	Boredom, stasis

Three of Cups	Celebration
Two of Cups	Partnerships
Ace of Cups	Beginnings, fertility, love

King of Cups

Character: King of Cups

Element: Air of the suit of Water

Astrological Sign/ Planet: Scorpio and Libra

General Interpretation: A charismatic man

The King of Cups is associated with The Emperor or the father symbol who brings authority, order, and structure. His domain is the emotions.

In this card, the King is sitting on a throne in the sea. He is comfortable despite the waves. Look at the sailing ship on the horizon, the big waves and the whit-gray sky.

Shell is the shape of his throne, and considering his obvious cool demeanor despite his isolation, he is reminiscent of Triton a Greek god of the sea who blew through a shell to control the waves.

He wears a fish amulet, which signifies faith and prosperity. A small fish can also be seen leaping from the left.

The water is gray, turquoise, and green - the many colors of the emotions. On his crown are red jellyfish and waves. The jellyfish is a reference to the King's zodiac reference, Scorpio.

The Upright King of Cups

The King of Cups usually comes up in readings to show the ideal romantic partner who is not afraid of intimacy while having stability and proper restrictions. It predicts fatherhood as well as children.

This card also foretells the need to settle a conflict, either within yourself or with a person at work or at home. You are not sure whether to be reasonable or creative - to follow your gut or conform with the status quo.

If you are in doubt, follow your intuition and allow your heart to rule. If you are in the negotiation table, remember to use empathy and your charm. If others feel that you are not engaged with them, communication will improve and they will lower down their defenses.

Keep in mind that if two or more Kings fall close together in a reading, they could be interpreted in the following ways:

- Two Kings indicate a genuine partnership
- Three Kings signify men of influence
- Four Kings may indicate a power struggle

The Reversed King of Cups

The reversed King of Cups reveals emotional weakness. If this is applicable to a person close to you, you may need to deal with someone who is volatile at the moment. This person may be timid or secretive. Fortunately this is only temporary and will change.

Another interpretation of the reversed card is a person with destructive behavior patterns and possibly addiction problems.

Queen of Cups
Character: Queen of Cups

Element: Water of the suit of Water

Astrological Sign/ Planet: Cancer and Gemini

General Interpretation: An intuitive woman

The Queen of Cups is associated with the Empress or the symbol of motherhood that brings abundance, kindness, and love.

She admires her treasure - a decorative golden chalice. Designed with a cross on top and two praying angels on the side it is a symbol of spirituality and faith.

The chalice is not open, which suggests the sacredness of the womb and life creation.

The card also portrays three water-babies - one holding a fish (symbol of prosperity), while the other two are sitting on each side of the throne like Gemini. The water-babies symbolize the maternal instinct of the Queen.

The Upright Queen of Cups

The upright presence of this card predicts positive influence of a sensitive and intuitive woman. She is compassionate and nurturing with developed emotional intelligence.

Her work may be creative, and she may also be attracted to the medical arts, caregiving, specific types of sales work, or research in non-mainstream topics.

Considering the Queen's natural empathy and sensitivity, this card urges you to choose your close friends carefully.

This card usually appears in readings to show the ideal female lover who is not afraid of intimacy while having the stability and proper limits. It also predicts motherhood and having children.

If two or more Queens fall close together in a reading, it indicates the following:

- Two Queens indicate rivalry
- Three Queens could mean friends who are willing to help
- Four Queens indicate women meeting up

The Reversed Queen of Cups

You may experience financial or emotional pressure. There could be jealousy in your personal relationships, and most negatively, this card in this position may show that someone is not loyal to you.

Knight of Cups
Character: Knight of Cups

Element: Fire of the suit of Water

Astrological Sign/ Planet: Pisces and Aquarius

General Interpretation: A proposal

The Knight of Cups is a proud one. With his gallant helmet adorned with the wings of the Greek God Hermes, he sits astride a dainty steed.

Poised and elegant-looking, this knight is dressed more for appearance than battle.

As conventionally knights all have a quest, the Knight of Cups aim to pursue love, which is symbolized by two elements on the card - the river flowing through the valley and the holy grail of love.

His blue armor is associated with the meaning of truth, which is also shown in the High Priestess. Meanwhile, the red fish decor on his tunic signifies passion and faith.

The Upright Knight of Cups

The Knight of Cups predicts an emotional period. There is a possibility that you will be enamored with a new love, experience more romance with your current lover, or other sweet things that can capture your imagination such as nature, beauty, or a temporary break from your work routine.

If you get two Knights in a reading, it could mean righteous friendship (or rivalry if at least one of the cards is reversed. Three knights signify a meeting of men, while four could indicate events being fast-paced and plenty of activity.

The Reversed Knight of Cups

The reversed Knight of Cups heralds disappointment - an offer that at initial glance seems perfect but does not materialize, leaving you feeling pushed out and confused.

As a person, the reversed Knight is unreliable and untrustworthy. He is committed on his quest, the sexual or romantic ideal, but has little desire to go beyond the honeymoon stage of a relationship. He may also be seeking for the thrill of new romance elsewhere, continuing the flow of control.

This card usually arrives in a reading to signify a lover who has issues with commitment and intimacy. His behavior may be unpredictable and inconsistent. But if challenged, he may protest that this is not an issue and try to avoid confrontation.

The best thing to do is to step away as this knight has little to offer other than being involved in high emotional ride.

Page of Cups
Character: Page of Cups

Element: Earth of the suit of Water

Astrological Sign/ Planet: None

General Interpretation: Romantic news

A whimsical page is holding a cup and looking at a fish inside. The fish seems to look at the page as if he is able to talk.

The fish is a symbol here of emotions and dreams that have materialized, so the young man is in deep contemplation. In Chinese mythology and folklore, the fish is a symbol of prosperity. In some pagan societies, the fish is also a symbol of fertility and often associated with the female genitals. The fish is also a symbol of the soul. Early Christians used the fish as a secret symbol during the Roman persecution.

However, the page in this card is not linked to any deep symbols. In fact, this card has a light atmosphere and playful vibe. The young man stands on dry land, and in the background there is flowing water.

The Page's clothes are decorated with water lilies, which is a traditional symbol of purity. This signifies that this page has a pure heart.

The Upright Page of Cups

The Page of Cups represents fun, good company, and sociability. Regardless of your age, this card heralds your feelings as a young at heart.

As Pages are natural heralds, this card brings good news about the emotional side of your life. This includes children, romantic relationships, and even money if this has a direct effect on your relationships.

In the romance side, this card shows a potential new partner. But this is not the Page of Cups himself because he is just a messenger. He is just sending you a message that love is about to come. While it is enticing to rush into a new romantic relationship, you may need to hold back a bit.

The Reversed Page of Cups

If reversed, the Page brings irresponsibility and frustration. Potential rewards may not materialize. You may feel that life is now filled with struggles.

As an individual, the reversed Page is not fully mature and always seeks attention. Therefore, it is not wise to depend on his perspective. He is only after his needs.

An additional interpretation of the reversed Page of Cups is intoxication. Maybe you are having too much fun that you are trying to ignore more important things in life.

This card urges you to relax down a bit and bring order to your life.

The Ten of Cups
Character: Ten of Cups

Element: Water

Astrological Sign/ Planet: Mars in Pisces

General Interpretation: Joy, family, prosperity

This card portrays an ideal family scene - father, mother, and their kids who are clearly having fun.

Their home is situated above the river, and from the river plain below. The couple looks at 10 bright cups in the sky floating with a rainbow. The sky is clear - no clouds can be seen, the trees are verdant, and the river is flowing.

The family is a wealthy one - depicted by their nice clothes - and they appear to be in victory over their accomplishment.

This is their kingdom. What can be happier than this place of contentment and security? The focus here is on the idea of a perfect life.

This is the perfect life - blessed by the vision of the 10 cups. The rainbow is a symbol of reward and hope. We can see the backs of the couple and even if the kids are busy with their game, they are happy while their parents are raising their arms in gratitude.

The Upright Ten of Cups

The Ten of Cups is one of the most positive cards of the Minor Arcana. It heralds the rewards of security and love of the family. It favors kids as an expression of love, and usually reveals that children will do well at school.

Therefore, the card heralds great happiness for families and couples or even close friends. In the workplace, this card shows harmony and peace for business partnerships and other important networks. Your strength is in unity and not competition.

In personal relationships, this is an emotional period but in a positive way. Connections built on trust and stability become even more supportive and rewarding.

Different generations of a family will help each other and put aside previous conflicts. It is also a typical card for forthcoming parties, weddings, and other important celebrations.

Communication between children and parents will grow stronger and be more satisfying.

If you are looking for a new home, the Ten of Cups shows this will materialize soon. You will also find the right property in the right location for your needs.

When it comes to projects, this card provides assurance that you will be rewarded for what you have worked hard. In your finances, the Ten of Cups is a positive indicator of prosperity that comes to you as a result of a well-deserved accomplishment.

The Reversed Ten of Cups

If reversed, the Ten of Cups retains much of its bright promise, but with some minor irritations.

You may need to resolve a concern within a family as your routine is affected. There is also a sense of discord in some relationships.

Your dreams of bringing your family and friends together may not be realized because of problems with communication. Equally, the need to keep up your appearances will prevent genuine understanding and communication.

Your friends may also bring problems under the influence of this reversed card. As such, a friend may step back from the circle.

But always take note that like all Minor Arcana cards, these effects are only temporary.

Nine of Cups

Character: Nine of Cups

Element: Water

Astrological Sign/ Planet: Jupiter in Pisces

General Interpretation: Happiness

Nine cups surround a man who is clearly radiant with pride. He shows off what he has in life - achievement and joy.

The cups are trophies - rewards for his previous efforts - on display for all to see. This is a card of genuine happiness. He fully enjoys his possession.

As the table is covered with a blue cloth, there is also a sense of celebration. The table set is ready to welcome a party. Certain of his role as a benefactor, it is the man's joy to share his wealth with others.

He is perfectly comfortable with this wealth signified by his posture on a low bench and wearing a cap and hose - both are red in color for joie de vivre and vitality.

The Upright Nine of Cups

This card is also known as the wish card because it heralds a dream come true. Whatever you dream for will soon materialize. Happiness comes from optimism, generosity, and prosperity alongside entertainment and parties.

In personal relationships, the Nine of Cups predicts new romance and genuine friendships. The feelings that you have nurtured in the past can now be expressed as others show their hearts. The period for waiting for love is over. It will be completely declared if love has grown.

As you feel more connected to your own heart, your friends will be closer to you. Other people will also respond when you fully live your truth. In the spirit of sharing, you will find it easier to connect with others as projects start and current work becomes more rewarding. This is a good time to appreciate all you have - to laugh and communicate.

The Reversed Nine of Cups

When reversed, ego steps in - and with it emotional disconnection and self-centeredness. This may manifest as smugness. More commonly in readings, the Nine of Cups reversed signifies narcissism. You are faced with the inability of other people to see beyond their own needs.

This influence may affect personal and business relationships that suffers as others forge ahead with their interests for short-term gain, which can leave you bruised.

Your creativity may also be affected at this time. Concentrate on sustaining balance and routine to help you explore these murky waters and hold onto your dreams and schemes.

This may not be the best time to nurture your ideas. However, this will not affect your worth or the viability of your ideas.

Eight of Cups

Character: Eight of Cups

Element: Water

Astrological Sign/ Planet: Saturn in Pisces

General Interpretation: Change, departure, emotional intelligence

Similar to the Moon card, this one portrays the combined sun and moon. Who will win? The moon (intuition and impulse) or the sun (the mind)?

It is evening - the moon's time. The figure is turning away from his comfortable surroundings under the light guided only by instincts.

The sun will have his time tomorrow. But for now, the man should go with the flow - following the water towards a new path. The hooded man has discovered a way to move forward. He has explored a pathway by the rocks that gives way to a safe riverbank. Here, he walks with purpose. This is reminiscent of the Hermit's staff or the Magician's wand - both are symbols of spiritual guidance.

The man's red cloak is a symbol of his capacity to manifest his intentions. There is also a sense that he has left the eight cups several moments ago. He fills the gap between the three cups on the top.

The Upright Eight of Cups

This is a time of restlessness and you may feel that something is missing. Personal and business relationships may appear in harmony from the outside. However, your intuition could be bothering you. The outcome may be a departure.

Conventionally, the Eight of Cups predicts that you will break an agreement or leave a situation that no longer gives you satisfaction.

Be wary of making hasty decisions. You should only move when you are certain that there's more you can contribute or gain. If the time is right, there's also less emotions that you would normally expect. Similar to the man on this card - moving under the hood, you may take your leave fast but silently.

The Reversed Eight of Cups

The reversed Eight of Cups urges you to take stock of what's holding you. Are you still clinging on to the past when you are really aware that your present circumstances must change?

This position reveals errors of judgement, so you either stay too long or you jump too soon. There's a possibility that you are not aware of the alternative ways to do things.

Timing is crucial now. You need to trust yourself that you will know the right time to move without too much pressure on yourself.

An additional interpretation of this card is feeling abandonment. You may feel confused as others are moving on from you with unceremonious pace.

Seven of Cups
Character: Seven of Cups

Element: Water

Astrological Sign/ Planet: Venus in Pisces

General Interpretation: Opportunities

Seven cups appear in the sky and an anonymous, dark figure seems to control or behold them. Every cup has its own cloud not like the one we see on the Ace of Cups.

But similar to the Ace of Cups, the cups in this card offers seven rewards. However, it is up to us to discover what is feasible.

At present, we are like the figure in the foreground - trying to understand the reality from fantasy. Each cup offers a unique symbol.

The first cup holds a male head with curly hair, which resembles the figure of Archangel Michael in the card of

Temperance. This signifies a higher force at work. This can also be interpreted as your own reflection, which is a sign of your future potential.

The small covered figure at the center cup signifies what is concealed and can be considered as a divine symbol. Maybe the hidden figure is sensing a divine plan that is yet to be revealed.

The third cup holds a snake, which stands for flattery and wisdom. This snake also appears in the Wheel of Fortune and the Lovers.

The fourth cup shows a fantasy castle, which symbolizes a fantastic spirit. Meanwhile, the fifth cup shows overflowing wealth.

In the sixth cup, we can see a laurel wreath that can also be seen in the Six of Wands card. But it is interesting to note that this cup has a shadowy skull image, which casts doubt on this positive interpretation.

The last cup holds a dragon or a salamander. Who knows if what you hear is true?

Generally, the seven images in the card reflect your imagination, sentiment, reflection, and contemplation.

The Upright Seven of Cups

The cards in this position heralds confusion and choices. Even though this card brings the possibility for great opportunities, these offers seem insubstantial.

At the moment, it is not yet clear what is fantasy and feasible, as everything feels up in the air, similar to the floating cups on the card itself.

Be discerning and figure out what you can about each potential way. But in the end you need to choose by paying attention to your emotions and instincts.

However, this is not a test of logic. Trust your gut and go with the flow. Avoid any rush action. In personal relationships, the card may show new doorways opening again as joint ventures improve.

This card is also known as the visionary card and presents the early stages of a new venture when anything is possible. Visions and dreams are additional meanings.

The Reversed Seven of Cups

The reversed appearance of the Seven of Cups has much the same interpretation as the upright card. But in this position, high emotions are usually at play.

You should be aware of the dangers of idealizing a situation and avoid a difficult truth. In personal relationships, this card predicts being deceived by looks and even betrayal.

Maybe this is not the right time for commitment. Stay away from being embroiled in emotional conflict. Step back until you are clear with your options.

Six of Cups
Character: Six of Cups

Element: Water

Astrological Sign/ Planet: Sun in Scorpio

General Interpretation: Old friendship, childhood memories, reconciliation, harmony

The two figures in this card are interesting - a girl dressed like an old woman and an overgrown child in a red cap holding a cup.

Four cups are standing in the foreground while another cup is standing on a stone podium decorated with a shield. The atmosphere of this card has a fairytale vibe. It is reminiscent of children's stories. Perhaps little red riding hood or even a prince awakening a princess.

This card reminds us of the past. The watchman and the tower on the left signifies protection while the flowers symbolize blossoming of spiritual and romance.

The Upright Six of Cups

This card heralds happy memories and a time to recall our childhood with fondness. If you have kids, they will help you to reconnect with your own childhood. You are also able to give your inner child freedom to have fun without worrying about your daily struggles.

This is a good time for good things coming from your past - reconnecting with your family and friends, reunion parties, or revisiting your old home. This card may predict a trip home or to a place with happy memories.

The past can also return to help you live peacefully in the present. In general, you will find the right balance in your relationships and enjoy a period of harmony and peace.

The Reversed Six of Cups

Nostalgia rules and you may remember previous events in a positive light. The card may also show you feeling trapped in the past as a way to avoid moving on.

A specific relationship should stay in the past instead of being rekindled. Unexpected messages or people may stir up old wounds, and if so, allow these memories to rest. People from your hurtful past have no place in your current life.

Five of Cups
Character: Five of Cups

Element: Water

Astrological Sign/ Planet: Mars in Scorpio

General Interpretation: Sorrow, leaving, and loss

A person covered in black shroud is mourning and contemplating three overturned cups. These cups are cast to the ground spilling water, wine, or blood.

A small house is situated above a river that flows under a bridge with two arches. This could be the dwelling that he has left behind, This symbolizes previous happiness and security that he is now separated from by the river. This body of water is reminiscent of the mythical river Styx, which divided the underworld from the world of the living.

The mourning figure is an uncomfortable terrain. The card depicts a place of sadness away from emotional security at least for the moment.

The Upright Five of Cups

This card is also known as the card of loss. It usually shows confusion and sadness due to arguments, frustrations, and breakup. It also reflects the temporary distance from a close friend or a family member who has caused you pain.

This card also applies to leaving home or a job before you are ready to do so. You need to force this deal with whatever life is giving you. This card may also refer to a loss of money or status. The gift of this card is that there's no mistaking what has happened because you also feel it deep within.

There's no going back at this point. However, all is not lost. You will be able to move onwards regardless of your situation. The two standing cups on the card shows the support of your family and friends.

This card also appears in a reading for bereavement and the natural sense of grief and loss that this brings. It is also an indicator that you or the recipient of the reading is reminiscing the past. You are probably trying to assimilate the old stress and grief so you can finally move on.

The Reversed Five of Cups

This card, along with the Devil card, are the only Tarot cards whose reversed interpretations are more positive than their upright counterparts.

The reversed Five of Cups reveal you have already undergoing the lowest point in a downward cycle. As a result, you are close to recovery and finally letting go of painful memories of the past.

Ready to move forward, you will be stronger than you were in the past. An additional interpretation of the card is meeting up with old friends and also coming back to life.

Four of Cups
Character: Four of Cups

Element: Water

Astrological Sign/ Planet: Moon in Cancer

General Interpretation: Boredom and restlessness

A young man is sitting under a tree, his legs and arms crossed. Three cups are set out in a row in the foreground. From a small cloud, a hand holds out another cup signifying a new beginning.

Even though the hand appears at his eye level, he is looking down. He refuses to recognize the cup being offered.

Disillusioned, the young man appears to be glancing frustratedly at the three cups resting on the grass as if to indicate that the fourth cup, regardless of what it may represent, is bound to be just more of the same old thing.

The young man's position is defensive, and he has set himself apart from the possibility of change and from his own emotions. Whatever his mood, the outlook is bright. The tree that provides him refuge is verdant.

He may enjoy the abundant life going all around him if he could just stand up and move around. Through this, the Four of Cups shows the possibility to see the light, to see that you are able to stand tall like a tree.

The Upright Four of Cups

If you are searching for a relationship, this card shows disenchantment. This usually appears if you have been damaged in the past and protect yourself with a checklist, immediately rejecting anyone who doesn't live up to your specific standards.

You may think that you are ready for love. However, there may be some issues in the past that you need to heal. If you are in a relationship, this card shows a tinge of boredom.

This could be a phase, and if so, it is probably time to add some romance into your life. You may find yourself staying in a relationship out of obligation. In home and work life, this card shows a static situation. You may feel bored with your job or you may need to make a positive change to your surroundings.

The Reversed Four of Cups

The interpretation of the reversed Four of Cups is basically the same as for its upright card but with a more intense dissatisfaction. You may be looking for change but don't yet know what you really want.

You may need to try new tactics at work and manage what you need to change in your environment or relationships. Try to express your needs now instead of locking them up. If the Four of Cups is reversed, the young man's crossed legs resemble the bent knee of the Hanged Man.

The Hanged Man's meaning is hanging around. Instead of waiting for change, the message is to take control and allow life to happen. Fortunately, this limbo is temporary - change is always possible.

Three of Cups
Character: Three of Cups

Element: Water

Astrological Sign/ Planet: Mercury in Cancer

General Interpretation: Friendship, family, abundance, celebrations

Three young ladies raise their cups in a toast. They are so close together that they almost appear as one figure, and as such they represent the three aspects of the goddess - the maiden, the mother, and the crone - the entire experience of a woman.

They are also seen as the three virtues in the Tarot signified by the colors of their robes. The woman in white is the maiden from the Strength card; the woman in red is Justice, and the woman in white and hold is associated with the Temperance. These three virtues provide us part of this card's interpretation - reunion, balance, and vitality.

The maidens are dancing barefoot and their robes are flowing. Completely engaged with life, two maidens raise their cups using their right hands and one maiden toasts using her left hand. The left hand is the hand of receiving, and the right hand is the hand of giving. So their poses shows they are able to both receive and give abundantly.

This card is also a card of material pleasures signified by the plentiful ripe fruits and the garden of flowers.

The Upright Three of Cups

The Three of Cups is the Celebration card. It heralds birthdays, weddings, christenings, anniversaries and other joyous occasions. This is a time for rewards and indulgence, to take pleasure in other's company, to have fund and be carefree.

There's also a flirtatious vibe in this card, so if you are looking for a relationship, you will soon be in an ideal situation and mood for a vibrant love.

The maidens in the card are raising their cups on a toast. This symbolizes abundance. But if you prefer wine than water, or you have a sweet tooth, you may be enticed to overindulge.

Regardless of your pleasure, this card finally reveals physical or emotional healing. Spending time with people who make you feel good could raise your energy and vibration levels.

The number three is also the number of creation. This signifies a creative time. Concentrate on bringing new ideas as whatever you do will be pleasurable and be well received. This is the time to allow your talent to shine.

The Reversed Three of Cups

If reversed, the Three of Cups may indicate an indulgence or flirtation gone too far with affairs and overbearing emotions. In established relationships, there may be a distance and a lack of understanding or unity.

Someone close may be egotistical and overly opinionated, and the dynamics of a close relationship - romantic or friendly - could be affected. Another common interpretation of the Three of Cups is emotional betrayal.

Your creativity can be affected, too, as you may experience creative block. It may be difficult to begin as you suffer a lack of support and motivation. Take a short break and resume working on your projects if you feel more grounded and less affected by the emotional demands of other people.

Two of Cups
Character: Two of Cups

Element: Water

Astrological Sign/ Planet: Venus in Cancer

General Interpretation: Old and new partnerships, love

Two figures (a maiden and a young man) face each other and offering each other with a cup. In the middle of them is an interesting symbol - a lion's head integrated with caduceus of Hermes.

The lion's head in this card can be interpreted as a symbol of protection as well as passion.

On the other hand, the caduceus is a rod with entwined two snakes. This is an ancient symbol of balance and negotiation associated with the Roman god Mercury (or Hermes among Ancient Greeks).

The young woman is dressed in the colors of the High Priestess (white and blue), while his partner is wearing boots and tunic that are similar to those of the man portrayed in the Fool card. Even the colors of his tunic (black, red, and yellow) are similar to the Fool.

The appearance of the intuition of the High Priestess and the beginnings of the Fool reveals a brand-new relationship in the cards. The young man wears a garland of red flowers, while the maiden is crowned with an olive garland. These two garlands signify love and success.

The couple's cup reveals that they are showing their emotions and the man's hand is reaching out to grasp the maiden's cup. This has sexual symbolism, as cups symbolizes the womb just as the wand symbolizes the male genitalia.

The Upright Two of Cups

The upright appearance of the Two of Cups represent love, partnership, peace, and harmony. In relationships, this card signifies a deeper commitment in a current relationship such as engagement or tying the knots of matrimony. There is a strong indication of marriage if this card appears with the marriage cards - the Ten of Pentacles or the Hierophant.

There's a strong connection between you and your partner, so your emotions are freely expressed and reciprocated. You feel full and satisfied. This card also heralds strong passions and new romance, which could be consuming for now.

This card also favors inspiring partnerships. Hence, this is a fortune card for getting together with a creative partner. Whomever you choose to partner with, the relationship will be mutually understanding and supportive.

The Reversed Two of Cups

The reversed Two of Cups predicts stress brought by your personal relationships. A new love interest may turn sour as your aspirations for romance are dissipated.

Moreover, this card asks you to depend on your intuition. Someone might be keeping an important secret from you, and the traditional interpretation of this card is infidelity.

Listen to your instincts. There's a reason behind your doubts, and it's best to openly express your fears instead of ignoring them.

If you are in a relationship, this card also indicate an unavoidable problem simply caused by stress from the workplace.

Ace of Cups
Character: Ace of Cups

Element: Water

Astrological Sign/ Planet: Pisces, Scorpio, Cancer

General Interpretation: Beginnings, relationships, love

One cup, offered by a hand that emanates from a cloud, is overflowing with water coming from five streams and pours into the lake below.

Water lilies grow on the surface of the lake. We can also see a white dove, which symbolizes peace. The bird is holding a wafer on its beak. The wafer is marked with the sign of the cross, which is a symbol of the Eucharist.

This card may symbolize the spark of the Divine, or the life force that enters the cup or the womb, for fertility at a physical, spiritual or creative level, reflecting the divine light.

Twenty six droplets appear to float around the cup, which is usually seen as a symbolism of semen. They resemble the form of dew drops on the Moon, the Tower, the Ace of Wand, and the Ace of Swords.

The Upright Ace of Cups

This card indicates love and important emotional events such as pregnancy, fertility, birth, and motherhood. Aside from heralding pregnancy, it also reveals that being a parent will take priority over your career.

In personal relationships, this card signifies falling in love, passion, and an important new partnership. In current relationships, it denotes love and support. Positive emotions flow. If you are working on a new project, this card heralds growth and creativity. Hence, it may be the time for things you enjoy, and you can witness them flourish.

A project you are really interested will start to bear fruit, so it is time to turn your ideas into reality and give them your full attention. This is also a positive card for spiritual development, so you will find yourself discovering a belief system or other significant ways to navigate your spirituality.

The Reversed Ace of Cups

When reversed, the Ace of Cups predicts creative block and pregnancy issues. You might be lacking in time and space to grow your relationships and projects, or you may be the one feeling ignored. You may be feeling drained because of the emotional demands from the people around you.

If you want to take a glimpse about new romance, unfortunately, the reversed Ace of Cups indicates confusion and disappointment. There's a high chance that a budding romance will not develop into something that will last.

Conclusion

Thank you for dedicating your energy and devotion as you have worked through the pages of this special book.

Throughout this journey, my goal is to provide you the knowledge you need to appreciate the Tarot.

But I also like to encourage you to read the cards your way. Try to develop your own style and enrich the connection with your cards.

While this beginner's guide may help you to begin your passion with the Tarot, and in some cases other areas of interest such as numerology or Kabbala, always remember that experience is the best teacher. You can find out more about those subjects and much more in my other books.

It is only through practice that you should trust the insights from the cards, and you can easily perform readings even without this book.

Lastly, I want you to keep the cycle of learning this ancient wisdom. You can choose to pass this along to your friends so they can also develop their intuition.

With these, we can all together appreciate our human existence and our world with more intimate perspective.

Thank you for taking the time to read the book.

Sofia Visconti 2019

Discover Psychic Tarot Reading, Tarot Card Meanings, Numerology, Astrology and Reveal What The Universe Has In Store for You

TABLE OF CONTENTS

Introduction

    What is Tarot?

    A brief history of Tarot Reading

CHAPTER ONE: How Does Tarot Work?

CHAPTER TWO: The most common tarot card spreads

    Most Common Tarot Layouts or Spreads

        The True Love Layout

        The Success Layout

        The Celtic - Cross Layout

CHAPTER THREE: A Guide To Your Tarot Deck

    The Major Arcana

    The Minor Arcana

CHAPTER FOUR: How to Use Your Tarot Cards

CHAPTER FIVE: Card Combinations, Patterns and Elemental Dignities

        Similar Meanings

    Elemental Dignities

        Qualities of Elements

        Elemental Dignities and its Relationships

CHAPTER SIX: Card Placements within a Tarot Spread

    Reading Cards in Tarot Spread Position

Three Card Spreads

CHAPTER SEVEN: Card Reversals and Timing

Card Reversals

Timing in Tarot Cards

Cards Denoting Transition or New Beginnings

Relationship Cards

CHAPTER EIGHT: The Meaning of Each Tarot Card

The Major and Minor Arcana

Court Cards

CHAPTER NINE: Reading a Tarot Card for the Day

CHAPTER TEN: Tarot as a Spiritual Doorway

A Cosmic String around Your Finger

Draw a Card and Cast a Spell

Om and Amen

CHAPTER ELEVEN: Bringing All Your Mystic Skills Together to Get the Results That You Want

CHAPTER TWELVE: Setting boundaries

CHAPTER THIRTEEN: Tarot Reading FAQ

CHAPTER FOURTEEN: Tarot Myths Busted

CHAPTER FIFTEEN: Summary…

Using Narratives or Storytelling in Tarot Reading

Shuffling Your Cards

Conclusion

INTRODUCTION

What is Tarot?

The Tarot consists of a deck of 78 cards that, over the centuries, absorbed the knowledge, stories, beliefs, histories, morals and life lessons of numerous cultures. Combine that with the all-powerful mind we possess, and we can use the Tarot to obtain vision into our lives, allow us to achieve, and strengthen us when we need to cope. Know that when reading the Tarot, we already know the answers to our own questions. However, those answers are concealed within our subconscious. The Tarot assists us in extracting that information.

There are 3 predominant tarot card systems which are generally used today - Marseille (around 1440), Rider-Waite-Smith (around 1909), and Thoth (around 1969). I personally like Rider-Waite-Smith and lean towards the Golden Dawn interpretive method.

Others may tell you that you don't need to know anything to read tarot. They say you can simply use your "psychic intuition." I humbly disagree. Critical theory is vital to accurately gaining a complete understanding of the Tarot.

A brief history of Tarot Reading

Tarot cards are said to have originated from Italy in the early 15th century. It was originally comprised of 21 trump cards and was created as a game for the nobles. Friars and conservative nobles during the era called the tarot cards as demonic cards because it contained characters or images that pertain to demons and death.

In the late 18th century, a cartomancer known as "Etielle" published a book containing the meaning of the cards and how they can affect the spirituality, destiny, and personality of a person. However, his version of tarot cards only contained 32 cards.

During the 19th century, Eliphas Levi correlated the tarot cards with the Hebrew Kabbalah. The new deck of tarot cards was comprised of 78 cards. Eliphas introduced the new deck as mystery cards that can answer every question of life. Since then, this new deck became the basic cards for a tarot reading.

Since the early tarot readers were almost precise on their readings and guidance, many believed that the cards could foretell a future event. Hence, until this day, many people still turn to tarot reading for guidance in their businesses, relationship, health, and decisions.

Chapter One
How Does Tarot Work?

Of course, the first question that many people ask is: Does a tarot reading really work? As explained above, not every reading works every time, but in general, both active readers and their subjects get a lot out of the process. It can be the subject of a long debate in another book if these tarot readings work because of the intuition of the reader or because of the tarot cards actually provide a connection to a universal store of knowledge and energy.

The concept of synchronicity seems to be what powers the tarot. Even though this term has gotten used in popular culture, a famous doctor of psychology first described it, and this doctor's name was Carl Jung. This is simply defined as two or even more events that appear to be related to each other but do not appear to have a link between why they happened.

In other words, events can be joined by meaning as well as by causality. When describing this concept back in the 1920s, Carl Jung said that there were no coincidences, and that is close to what tarot scholars believe. It is similar to somebody shrugging their shoulders at a series of unlikely events that seem related and saying, Stuff just happens.

This explains what happens when a particular way and unique way of shuffling the deck produces each card that fits into the pattern. It is also what happens when all of the cards merge together into an entire pattern. Practitioners believe that the phenomenon of synchronicity creates exactly the right spread of tarot cards to produce the appropriate pattern of symbols and meanings that answer the questions presented to the deck. Are the questions asked of the deck, the tarot card reader, the universe as a whole or the subject herself? That is for each individual who studies the tarot to decide.

In other words, the graphical symbols, card numbers, and their inherent meanings reflect the powerful minds of the readers and the subjects. This language of symbols, the language that the cards speak can talk to the minds of the reader and subject in a way that words cannot.

It is not hard to speculate that the ability to understand symbols is even older than the ability to understand words. Probably, the first words were actually symbols. It is certainly true that the oldest known languages in the world were written down with images instead of phonetic letters.

People are able to grasp the inner meaning of the symbols that represent their meanings in words. By doing this, they learn to understand what the deck is trying to tell them truly. In fact, the deck is probably just a pile of cardboard. That is like saying the Declaration of Independence is just a piece of old paper. It is the meaning that human minds can take away from the symbols on the cards that makes them work so well.

Interpretation Of Symbols In Occult Tarot

Each card has a symbol and charts that diagram some general ways to interpret them. However, the real interpretation comes from the reader, and each one is unique. Cards may be interpreted on their own, by their position in the spread, and also through the filter of the reader's own experiences.

This means that each reading is unique. Also, two readers might interpret the same patterns and symbols in different ways. Does this mean that one of them is wrong? As mentioned above, there are failed readings. However, these are actually very rare. It is more likely that both readers have different perspectives about the issues, and they may each receive somewhat different images because of this.

If one person says a glass is half full and another says the class is half empty, does that mean

That one is wrong? No, each of these people is simply expressing a different general outlook on the same glass with the same amount of liquid in it. In this same way, two readers may give different readings, and both be right.

Again, the future is not immutable. The subject usually has great control over the outcome, and the cards may get proven wrong. Hopefully, this is because the subject received great insight from reading and learned to approach some situation or challenge in her life in a more positive way. If the tarot contributed to this, but the reading did not actually foretell the future, does this make the tarot wrong? No, the tarot worked exactly the way it was intended to.

The final concept from this section is based upon reminding readers that the tarot is only a deck of cards. Some may be plain, and some may be very beautiful. Skilled artists craft some decks, but others are made at home. Either way, the outcome of reading doesn't really say much about a pile of cards. It says something about the reader, but it says more about the subject who approaches the tarot for answers to important questions.

There are plenty of instruction guides to help readers learn to use tarot cards. Volumes have been written. Simple guides to meaning can be found in books or even on the Internet. But these instruction guides are all meaningless on their own without the talent and intuition of the reader and the cooperative insight of the questioner.

Mainly, the tarot is not an instruction guide. It doesn't provide a fix-it guide for people with problems. However, it is intended to provide insight into problems, how these problems arose, and possibly, how to avoid the worst consequences of them in the future.

Chapter Two

The most common tarot card spreads.

In this chapter, you'll learn the most common tarot spreads or layouts for beginners and also for expert tarot readers. Be reminded though that this is listed in no particular order. You'll also get to learn the meaning of each spread so you can easily connect the cards and be able to answer your client's question more accurately. It's up to you to determine which spread might work best for any type of reading; it's probably best to learn them all so you can have the chance to see what's more appropriate for you and your subjects. Now, let's lay down the cards on the table!

Most Common Tarot Layouts or Spreads

The True Love Layout

This spread or layout focuses on a person's relationship, but not just about one's romantic relationship (although it's the most common topic among seekers). It's also used to evaluate a person's physical, spiritual, and emotional connection to their current or potential partners. It's a six card spread, and the pattern signifies a certain interpretation.

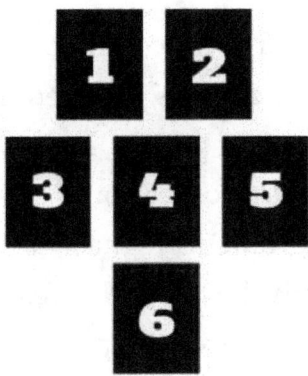

#1 Card: Signifies how the seeker feels about the current relationship that he/she is in. It also includes one's outlook towards the relationship.

#2 Card: Signifies the seeker's partner (either spouse, boyfriend/girlfriend) and his/her feelings about the relationship as well as one's expectations

#3 Card: Represents the connection or common characteristics of the seeker and his/her partner

#4 Card: Represents the qualities of strength in the relationship

#5 Card: Represents the weakness qualities of the relationship and the things both parties should improve on

#6: Represents how the relationship is going to go or what needs to be done to maintain or perhaps create a more meaningful connection with one another.

The Success Layout

Obviously, this type of spread is concern about an individual's successes in terms of career, dreams, or even in oneself. This kind of layout will also help a person in how to overcome certain challenges and could also get some advice on how to achieve a resolution to a problem. It may also represent the things an individual already has like the resources or skills that are available. It's also a five – card spread with this layout:

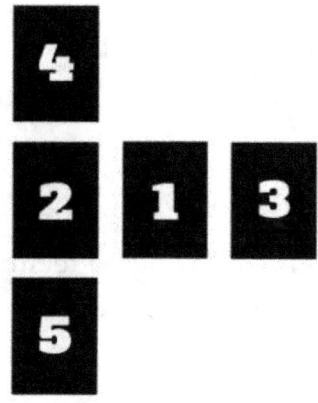

#1 Card: Represents the main challenge or problem of the seeker

#2 Card: Represents the complications from those challenges

#3 Card: Denotes some factors that the seeker needs to know which are affecting the current situation

#4 Card: Signifies the people or ideas that could make the seeker grow to achieve a certain goal

#5 Card: Indicates what the seeker needs to do to achieve a goal, avoid failure as much as possible, and become successful in an endeavor.

The Celtic - Cross Layout

The Celtic – Cross spread is one of the most complex types of tarot reading but it's perhaps one of the most original layouts, and it has been used for many centuries. The layout's versatility has been helpful in assessing complicated queries because it can be read in different ways depending on the card's combinations and patterns. This kind of layout basically focuses on the seeker's issues as well as the outside factors that are at play. This type of layout may be quite hard to understand, especially for beginners, but of course, practice can make you better. This is a 10 – card spread with this

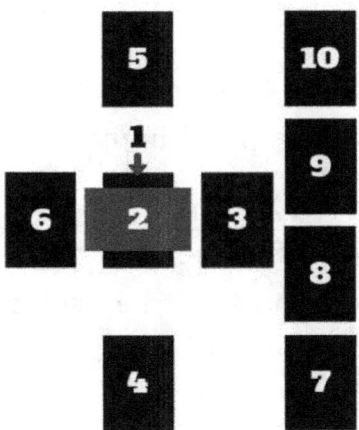

layout:

#1 Card: Represents the seeker's current situation

#2 Card: It represents what's holding a person back or what is helping him/her

#3 Card: Focuses more on the seeker's true desire that he/she may be unaware of, as well as the subconscious influences that ultimately affects his/her life

#4 Card: Represents the past events and issues that are still bothering the seeker

#5 Card: Focuses on one's conscious desires and the goals that are very important for the seeker. It can also tell where the person should place his/her energy and how one should use that energy to accomplish an objective.

#6 Card: Represents one's path – either positive or negative. If it's particularly negative, the card in this placement can also tell the seeker how he/she can avoid it or bounce back from it.

#7 Card: Represents the seeker's attitude, ideals, and actions

#8 Card: Represents the kind of energy that the seeker gets from the people surrounding him/her and if this energy is helpful or not

#9 Card: Also known as the revelation card; it denotes that there are things that should not be neglected and one must pay attention to such things because it can have a huge impact in the current or possible situations.

#10 Card: This is the final outcome of a situation, and it is also related to the #5 card. It will tell the reader and the seeker if the energy in a particular issue is complementing or conflicting one another.

Chapter Three
A Guide To Your Tarot Deck

In this section, we'll examine all 78 cards that make up a standard Rider-Waite tarot deck. These interpretations are a product of accepted knowledge about the cards, combined with my own experience working with them. Rather than take them as definitions etched in stone, view them as starting points. You don't need to memorize these definitions. In fact, you can even skip this section for now and start working with the cards in section 3.

This section can serve as an aid when you struggle to find meaning with a card. From here, you can develop your own understanding, which no book can supply. The tarot's value lies in connecting it to your own life and consciousness.

The Major Arcana

The 22 cards of the Major Arcana can be viewed as a sequence through life. This has some appeal for its elegance, but it can also be a limitation. We need not feel obligated to respect this classification. What is generally agreed upon is that these cards are universal experiences. Some of them may dominate your personality. Some of them are people and places that show up again and again. Whoever and wherever you are, these cards can be found on any given day.

0: THE FOOL – The Fool stands outside of time and the universe, and so he is symbolized by the number zero. But he is inextricably drawn to time and the world of life. He recognizes the vanity and illusory nature of existence. Is he enjoying the view, or is he about to step over the cliff? From his perspective, seeing the emptiness of all being, it is one and the same. He is ready to travel in any direction. He is the unborn, the infinite, and not yet bound by any laws of physics, psychology, or government.

1: THE MAGICIAN – Like the prime agent of creation, the Magician takes responsibility and acts, directing the flow of events. Creation, as symbolized by the wand he holds high, is his primary method for inducing magic. However, he has the other elements at his disposal at any time. He unites heaven and earth (note his gestures) and is a channel for the energy that flows through him. He is tied to the infinite and the universe itself (note the infinity sign above his head), and his action is an act of surrender to his higher self. Any action he takes works **through** him.

2: THE HIGH PRIESTESS – The most intuitive sense within us, the High Priestess is a repository of everything that religion can only hint at. She is the unspoken space between thoughts. She is pure love and compassion as emanated by the universe.

3: THE EMPRESS – Unlike the High Priestess, the Empress is all that is earthly and motherly. She is nature, motherhood, the feminine, abundance, the harvest, and the most comfortable aspects of this world.

4: THE EMPEROR – The Emperor is the masculine principle. He is action, confidence, firmness, and decisiveness. He can represent conquest, war, or other confrontation. He is seated, however, and if the situation is to his liking, then he remains firm in his position.

5: THE HIEROPHANT – As a religious figure, the Hierophant (unlike the High Priestess) represents the outer layers of spirituality. He is custom, orthodoxy, formality, ceremony, and tradition. He shows up when a formal situation or procedure is required or about to take place. You can try to fight against these traditions if you think they are nonsense, but like the church, they have a lot of staying power. Sometimes it is easier to accept a tradition, and sometimes you must fight it.

6: THE LOVERS – This card deals with attachment to an outcome. The lovers wish to be united, but it is ultimately in the hands of the larger forces of the universe. The feminine principle is more willing to accept this, while the masculine principle is more concerned with itself and its own power of agency.

7: THE CHARIOT – The Chariot is a card that seeks to balance the masculine and feminine principles. It requires to give and take. Equate this card with the yin and yang symbol of Taoism. A strong charioteer can keep the situation under control. This might indicate the need for better management of a situation.

8: STRENGTH – The Strength card is about using your higher mental faculties to control your lower instincts. These urges include the seven deadly sins of pride, greed, lust, envy, gluttony, wrath, and sloth. All of these sins come from attachment to the individual ego.

9: THE HERMIT – The Hermit is the wise man. Although we think of hermits as isolated from society, this card often turns up when it is time to go into the world and offer the wisdom you have learned. The Hermit is humble and knows that his light will light the way for others. Light does not

Argue – it simply shines.

10: WHEEL OF FORTUNE – The Wheel is a key moment when the potential for reward is great. It may also lead to adversity, but it is primarily a positive sign, in my experience. The key is giving up attachment to a particular outcome. Often good comes from unexpected directions, and in forms, we hadn't expected.

11: JUSTICE – As you sow, so shall you reap. You get what you pay for. The consequences of your past actions are now experienced, for better or worse. Have you lived with integrity? Have you lived up to your ideals? Few of us do, so this card usually involves atonement or retribution for past acts. However, if you have done well, it can also bode well.

12: THE HANGED MAN – As this man is hung in a torturous position, he has an **aha** moment. This state recalls that of the Fool, outside of the universe. But the Hanged Man is still enmeshed in the physical world and his journey.

Nevertheless, he has awoken to the true nature of his existence and the insubstantial nature of this world.

13: DEATH – Despite the dark image we have of death, this card rarely means a **natural** death. More commonly, it indicates the death of a lifestyle or personality and a chance to be born again. Following on the heels of the Hanged Man, Death is an opportunity to reassess how you've been living. Ironically, it is a moment of new growth. Awareness of death allows you to live truly.

14: TEMPERANCE – With a new paradigm comes new feelings and new experiences. With one foot on land and one foot in the water, the angel of Temperance tries to manage and make sense of these new states. He is still dabbling and not fully immersed, cautiously approaching the newness of the world.

15: THE DEVIL – The Devil is the individual ego and its burning desires. This card is the dark inversion of the Lovers card. Who is enchained by the Devil? Humanity. Our human-level mind, our sexuality, our hunger, and all that we cling to. The man and woman have been enchained by their consciousness. The devil is a sense of lack, absence, emptiness, and division.

16: THE TOWER – The Tower is a great destabilization of life in the material world. Whatever you have constructed in this world may be taken from you in an instant. It may not necessarily occur when this card comes up, but it will happen someday. This card is the moment when you remember the transitory nature of the world. The crisis of this card occurs when the material world is used as the basis for your life. This card says Anything that can be taken from you is not truly yours.

17: THE STAR – The Star is the entryway to dreams, hallucinations, and the unshackling of your spirit from your individual ego. Emotion rules this realm, not logic. It may also indicate an intuitive solution rather than an analytical plan.

18: THE MOON – The Moon is a full immersion into the realm of dreams. The ego is nearly gone at this point. The wolf, scorpion, and even the domesticated dog have surrendered to the larger power of nature and the universe. We all possess this intuitive understanding of life.

19: THE SUN – The Sun is the awakened being. He sees that all life emanates through him as love and that all characters in the universe are united by the light. To become light is to transcend time and exist in a state of bliss.

20: JUDGMENT – Judgment is when you see your own identity as an object. And yet, there is still you to witness it. But all personality is disconnected from the experience – there is only the sense of I AM.

21: THE WORLD – Finally, the World. There is no sense of individual identity separate from what is. There is simply THIS. Time is absent. Space is absent. This might be likened to whatever happened before the Big Bang, or where you were before you were born. From the tiniest subatomic particles to the largest universal scales, everything is encased in a single being. This state is completely alien from day-to-day life... and yet, it is always with us. It cannot leave us, or it wouldn't be the World. From the perspective of the World, there is nothing to be done, nothing that can be done, and nothing to fear (since you are the only person in the room). There is no sense of right or wrong. The universe and all of the time can be viewed as an artifact that hovers like a piece of finished art. Time has become a product of the human brain, from which you are disconnected.

The Minor Arcana

Unlike the Major Arcana, which focus on individual states of consciousness, the Minor Arcana are concerned with specific people, events, situations, modes of intelligence, and external experience.

The four suits correspond to the four major cognitive bits of intelligence: emotional intelligence (cups), creative intelligence (wands), logical intelligence (swords), and sensory intelligence (pentacles).

SWORDS

Swords (along with Wands) seem to separate us from other animals. While some animals can reason and use tools in very basic ways, humans have taken logic and design to a completely different level. Why do humans hold the fate of the Earth in their hands? There are more insects than humans on Earth. There are larger, more powerful animals like elephants and whales. There are faster animals like cheetahs and wolves. But it is our ability to think and the reason that allows humans to dominate planet Earth.

Swords is the suit of logic and organization. Here are some examples of Swords at work:

Using a map.
Looking up how to do something online.
Learning the rules of a game or sport.
Setting an itinerary.
Making an appointment.
Designing a cabinet.
Writing the code for a computer program.
Having a business meeting to review the previous quarter.
Using a tool like a compass or a ruler.
Writing an essay.
Engaging in a debate in a reasoned way (not emotionally arguing).
Following a recipe to make a cake.

Here are my interpretations of the Swords cards:

THE ACE OF SWORDS: The bursting forth of logic, planning, and design. This may come at a moment when you've been immersed in one of the other elements, and now it is time for more effective control. The sheer power of reason and design should not be taken lightly. It can completely alter the course of a life or a society. Because of its power to shape and cut through the other elements, swords often dominates, hence the crown. Surrounding the sword are six of the Hebrew letter **Yod**. This letter is associated with humility. To use the sword of reason without humility is to court disaster. As with all power, if it is based on the individual and desire, it will bring destruction. If it is based on love, the greater good, and harmony, it will bring prosperity.

2 OF SWORDS: The querent is safely protected by a sword in each hand. But she cannot see. Furthermore, she has the sea of emotions behind her, but she cannot experience it in this fearful, guarded state. This is a conservative, reactionary position. It may be safe, but eventually, your arms will tire, and you will grow bored. On the other hand, if you've been experiencing too many emotions, this guarded position might be what you need right now. But it is no way to live your whole life.

3 OF SWORDS: This may be the time to let logic dominate emotion. But whose emotions? If they are yours, are you willing to experience the pain or heartbreak? If it is someone else, be aware that you are choosing logic over love. Are you prepared to live with this?

4 OF SWORDS: Although a member of the swords family, this card is a state of meditation. It may be time to pause as you make plans. Instead, daydreaming and rest may allow the intuitive mind to work. If you try to force logic, it can backfire. Sometimes it's best to rest and put the conscious mind aside. When you return to a challenge, you will handle it better.

5 OF SWORDS: Checkmate! This arrogant fellow has outwitted his peers. He doesn't seem to care about their

feelings. A sword is a great divider. It does not build communities, and although you

May enjoy the victory a sword allows, you will not always be the winner. Remember, those who live by the sword shall die by the sword.

6 OF SWORDS: I call this card, moving on. This may come at a time when your plans have fallen through. This forlorn trio glides over a muted sea of emotion. They have their swords with them, but they serve no purpose here. The swords might even block their view. This is no time for planning. It is a time of recovery. It may be best to leave a situation and regroup at a later time.

7 OF SWORDS: This sneaky fellow is confident he's about to pull a fast one on the people he's left behind. And he just might! After all, look at all the weapons he's got. However, you can only hold two swords at any given time. Unless he has friends to wield those extra swords, what good will they serve? Or perhaps he merely hopes to disarm his foes. Note how he carries the swords by the blades – not the best way to handle a weapon! This could signify a person handling a device, weapon, or plan out of their league. Also, what happens if he trips?

8 OF SWORDS: Logic has fenced this person in. The trickle of water at her feet is the only source of joy. It might be better to follow that emotion to a larger body of water. But first, she needs to break free of her bindings. It might be necessary to use those swords first (logical planning), and then get away

from them. We often can't escape from our situation immediately, and some planning may still be required if we hope to find a more fulfilling situation.

9 OF SWORDS: Are you noticing a theme of despair in the sword cards? This fellow, with all his weapons, is besieged by nightmares in the cold dark. He might use his swords like a ladder to climb his way out, or he could leave them behind altogether. But it's so hard to leave our habits behind, even when they trap us.

10 OF SWORDS: The ultimate ruination of a situation dominated by swords. Your eyes face the emotions that you sought, but you are now pinned down (and perhaps destroyed) by your unerring devotion to logic.

THE PAGE OF SWORDS: The initial stirring of plans. When a sword is first held, its weight and power are incredible. The youth looks around and sees what he might accomplish with the power of a plan.

THE KNIGHT OF SWORDS: Action! With more coordination than any other knight, the knight of swords is a terrific opponent indeed. When he focuses, he can overcome nearly any foe.

THE QUEEN OF SWORDS: The queen has used her sharp mind to cut a strong place for herself in the world. But there is a grayness to her being; her emotions choked out of her. Her place is firm, but she is almost a statue.

THE KING OF SWORDS: The king of swords has disarmed all his opponents and has complete power. His view of the world is elevated, and he has a strong pillar behind him. Anyone wishing to overcome him has their work cut out for themselves. Yet despite all this, he is an emotionally hollow creature who can barely manage a grin.

CUPS

As the carrier of emotional intelligence, cups are all about feelings. Not hot or cold, or physical pain or pleasure, but the more powerful sensation of **emotion**. Like breathing, our emotions happen even if we stop thinking about them. But also like breathing, you can take conscious control of your emotions. Here are some examples of Cups at work:

You feel butterflies as you kiss someone for the first time.

Your investments lose a large amount of money, and you feel like you just got punched in the stomach.

Someone tells a silly joke, and you laugh uncontrollably.

You take a much-needed vacation to Hawaii and feel a sense of bliss as you float in the water.

A sad movie brings you to tears.

You miss your subway train by seconds and feel frustrated.

Eating apple pie reminds you of your grandmother's cooking, and you get a warm, fuzzy feeling.

Your pants fall down, and you blush with embarrassment.

Watching the evening news makes you bitter about the world.

Here are my interpretations of the Cup cards:

THE ACE OF CUPS: Look at the ambiguously left/right hand. Look at the unnatural shape of the water falling from the cup. Water doesn't fall like this! It actually goes **up** before curving down. And the streams are so tightly focused. This card represents an opportunity for emotion, and when emotion comes through, it is not in a general way. It is clearly defined. All emotions are based on the emotion of universal awareness, the seeing into the pure undivided love that is the universe sometimes called **agape**. The material world rests upon the emotions in the form of the lily pads. Peace (in the form of the dove) delivers balance and symmetry to the emotions.

2 OF CUPS: In its most basic differentiation, the universe splits into masculine and feminine principles. The masculine is active. The feminine is passive. But this card typically symbolizes a partner or goal that is unwilling to work with the querent. Do not lust after results, as Aleister Crowley says. This card often comes up when you desire something to happen, but the universe isn't giving it to you. Let go and surrender to the universe.

3 OF CUPS: A harmonious interaction with the parts of the universe. This card looks like a party because it is. When a group of individual emotions is in sync, what else would you call it? Just remember that all parties come to an end. The participants have their attention on the emotions they're experiencing. But notice: They are surrounded by plant life, the inevitable presence of the material world.

4 OF CUPS: The querent has three cups before him. They are either empty or not to his liking. This has left him in a

disgruntled state. But he is being offered another cup that could satisfy him! He is either blind to it or refuses to give it his attention. Are you so focused on your losses that you ignore new possibilities for happiness?

5 OF CUPS: Here, the querent is even deeper within his regrets about the past. There are always new possibilities for expansion, but you must face them and be willing to move beyond the past. Also, notice that a river lies just beyond the querent. You may have lost the emotions you've known in the past, but there are always new joys to sustain you. They will take different forms and may not

Be as exciting or have the same flavor as before, but they will sustain you. The old forms are always changing. Clinging only brings despair.

6 OF CUPS: The emotions of this card are simple, nostalgic, or childish. They are based on a child's view of the material world (symbolized by cups full of flowers), uncomplicated by the larger burdens of life. Both the boy and the girl have their vision blocked by this view of the world. Yet, like all aspects of our awareness, it is invented. It may be enjoyed for what it is.

7 OF CUPS: This is a card of possibilities, of forking paths. Each will lead you to a slightly different emotion. When this card comes up, ask yourself: Which cup is my attention being drawn to? Also, do not assume that any of the cups are bad or good. You do not know who lies beneath the covered figure. You do not know if the snake or dragon are allies or enemies.

This card will teach you that you assign meaning to situations. Also, notice that the querent's form is shadowy. Without a person to reflect on them, these objects can carry no emotion.

8 OF CUPS: This card always makes me think of a retreat from emotion. The cups have been left behind. The traveler has crossed a stream and is hiking into the realm of sensory materialism. The dreamy qualities of the moon may still be overhead, the water may be nearby, but the querent is trying to stay on firm ground. There are many times when it pays to turn your emotions down. Similarly, there are times when emotions are required. Consider which is best for the current situation.

9 OF CUPS: I like to call this card the merchant of feelings. Like a store owner, he has access to a (nearly) full range of emotional experiences. But they sit behind him. He is not using them. He can access them at any time, but he is glad just to help others find the emotions they seek (and profit from the transaction). He is firmly grounded and content, and in a very powerful position.

10 OF CUPS: Unlike card 9, card 10 is fully experiencing the spectrum of emotions. It is exhilarating and joyous. It may be likened to a supernatural experience. Like rainbows, understanding the science behind your emotions does not lessen their effect.

THE PAGE OF CUPS: The page is the simplest stirring of emotion. It will make the querent curious for more and is hardly satisfying.

THE KNIGHT OF CUPS: The feeling behind the knight is noticeably stronger than the page. For me, the knight cards are usually the point when a call to action takes over. A person feeling this emotion cannot suppress it (as can be done with the page). This card may be compared to overwhelming hunger for an emotion. If that desire can be fulfilled, excellent. If not, the knight will experience frustration.

THE QUEEN OF CUPS: The queen's emotional state is nearly overwhelming. The water is nearly at her toes. But she is still on land. Nevertheless, this level of emotional involvement is either blissful or hellish, depending on the circumstances.

THE KING OF CUPS: The king represents the purest feeling of a complete emotional experience. There is no logic, creativity, or sensory awareness. There is only pure emotion. He is completely afloat on turbulent waters. If he is a strong king, he will survive and eventually reach land. If he is weak and the water grows too rough, the emotion may drown him.

PENTACLES (DISKS)

The material world, which we know through our senses, is the realm of the Pentacles. It is the most grounded of suits, and thus associated with the element earth. If you want to deal with the practical, the pragmatic, and the sensible, then Pentacles are for you. All that you find in the world before you mask it with your thoughts and feelings is the domain of pentacles. This suit also deals with responsibility – think of boy scouts and girl scouts and their emphasis on survival skills.

Here are some examples of Pentacles:

Rain falls on a sidewalk.

You sweep the dust off your floor.

Two cars collide.

The power goes off in your house.

A volcano erupts.

You itch your leg.

Dominos fall.

Your freezer turns water into ice.

A factory assembles a ship.

You lift weights at the gym.

Cats are meowing in an alley.

A flower blossoms.

Here are my interpretations of the Pentacles cards:

ACE OF PENTACLES – The Ace cards are typically the pure manifestation of the element. With Pentacles, this looks like the Garden of Eden. Human consciousness has not yet intruded upon the earthly realm, and nature is in a pure state.

2 PENTACLES – A person with his hands full, overwhelmed by life. Not only are his hands tied by his world, but his emotions (the water behind him) are messy. This is not a person enjoying life, but a person constrained by it.

3 OF PENTACLES – This card is about collaboration to make something in the physical world. The planner and the priest oversee the worker. All three people have different visions for what they are creating, but compromises are necessary for collaboration.

4 OF PENTACLES – At this stage, the man has a firm grip on his material reality. His world has been managed and controlled. This control may be satisfying, or it may lead to his undoing.

5 OF PENTACLES – This is a stage of physical suffering. Perhaps you lost your job, or your house has been repossessed, or you broke your leg. The loss is material, in some sense. Notice that these two people are outside the church, signifying their spiritual emptiness. The loss may be physical, but they always have access to the spiritual realm.

6 OF PENTACLES – This is a stage of prosperity, and giving back to others. But as you do so, you remember how much you have. You're careful not to give **too** much away. You may be **lending** and keeping a strict account of all you give. This could be a prosperous businessman, or affluent parents providing for a child.

7 OF PENTACLES – Much work has been done, and this has led to a material harvest. It may be savings for retirement or other stockpiling of wealth. It may be a house acquired after years of hard work or some other form of security.

8 OF PENTACLES – This card is a position of order and connection to the world. The man knows his role and fills it. He is satisfied with his work and has no time for frivolous activity.

9 OF PENTACLES – This card is a position of comfort and satisfaction, a period of great success with life. This person may, however, be disconnected from the community at large.

As often is the case, when we are happy, we forget those who are miserable.

10 OF PENTACLES – This person is extremely comfortable in the world. Perhaps he has even retired from the hustle and bustle of the world at large. Others may view him as obsolete or in decline. His comfort is assured, but he may be dissatisfied with his existence like there is still something lacking, or more to live.

PAGE OF PENTACLES – The Page of Pentacles is like a child in nature. It could be a person leaving school or the office after many years. It is a confrontation with the physical stuff of existence.

KNIGHT OF PENTACLES – The knight is much more comfortable with the concrete nature of life. This could be a national park ranger or just someone who can look beyond the signs and symbols of culture and experience what is actually present in the world.

QUEEN OF PENTACLES – The passive aspects of the physical world. The queen is all that is reserved and quiet in the world. She is a gentle breeze, the peace, and the quiet of nature. Things are always happening at some level, but through the queen, they are most relaxed.

KING OF PENTACLES – The king is in full control of his world. He completely understands how the physical processes of life and nature function. He may also signify great wealth, comfort, and abundance. He does not get caught up in the turbulence of emotions.

WANDS

Wands are the suit of creativity, intuition, and spontaneity. A magician's wand is a channel for energy, and your imagination does the same thing. Organizing this energy is the work of swords and pentacles, but the energy itself flows through the wand. Its element is fire, which radiates heat. But fire can also get out of control and destroy.

Here are some examples of Wands at work:

You paint a picture of the first thing that comes to your mind.
You make up a song on the piano.
A story idea comes to you from out of the blue.
A vision of your dream house appears effortlessly in your mind.
You are interviewing candidates for a job, and you pick one intuitively, not logically.
You have vivid dreams while sleeping.
You imagine the best way to decorate your home.
You write a bucket list of the fun things you want to do.
You imagine a new possibility for software that has never been done before.
You come up with different uses for a space in your community.

Here are my interpretations of the Wands:

ACE OF WANDS – The ace is the eruption of a suit into the querent's life. Which is not to say that the element was absent beforehand, only that the element is making its presence felt in a larger way. With wands, this is the opening of the imagination, the realm of the possible. Imagination is a playful place full of possibility, and it is best approached with a child's attitude of adventure.

2 OF WANDS – This is early in the stage of imaginative or spiritual exploration. The man is secure in his castle, but he sees the potential in the world all around him. This is a card of infinite possibilities that recalls the phrase, Who dares, wins.

3 OF WANDS – This is a more challenging position for the querent. A desert surrounds him. On the other hand, the man uses his wands as strong support. His inner strength may make up for a lack in the outer world.

4 OF WANDS – Humanity is seen from a distance. A celebration, party, or drunken feast is taking place, but the querent is distant. How does humanity appear to you here? Do you see them as good? Or do you despise them and want to keep your distance? Whatever the case, you are adding to the scene's texture. Notice how wands, connected with spiritual energy, are united with plant life (pentacles, or material energy).

5 OF WANDS – In this card, we see a clash of worldviews. The boy who holds his wand the highest is the one most removed from the battle. If you enjoy argumentation, you may want to stay in the battle – otherwise, it may be beneficial to step away. True creativity does not worry about rewards or esteem from the world. It is only interested in the act of creation.

6 OF WANDS – This is a card of victory and smooth sailing (perhaps after the contention of the previous card). The horse's rider may be smug and satisfied, but he is hardly in a position to create.

7 OF WANDS – This is a card of energetic creation. Unlike card 5, the querent is in a better position to operate in the world. Here, his creativity is based on responding to the work of others. Much like dancing, this kind of creation is impossible alone.

8 OF WANDS –Something is about to be determined, as these wands are up in the air. All four elements are in this card. Air is already acting upon the energy of the wands, trying to organize it. Earth and water wait to see how the wands shall land. A creative endeavor may be underway, and for

Now, it cannot be stopped.

9 OF WANDS – The act of creation has been accomplished, but this is not a creative card. The work is done; the man looks at his accomplishments. If he rests on his laurels and becomes transfixed by his past work, he will be unable to create anew. He must break new ground or else the wands will act as a cage.

10 OF WANDS – Here the querent is trying to move forward creatively. He still clings to his past. He sees his future through his previous endeavors. He is unwilling to let go. For creativity to be free, it cannot be held to yesterday's rules. On the other hand, the querent may be taking his ideas to sell to a company, for example. That may be appropriate now – just

recognize that it will not be a **creative** act, and it is better handled by the intellect of swords.

THE PAGE OF WANDS – This is the young artist or spiritual novice attempting a new creation. The work may be unimpressive at this point, but **he** is impressed with himself. Did this really come from him? Many people dabble with creation at this level and take it no further.

THE KNIGHT OF WANDS – The knight has honed his craft and is about to release his energy into the act of creation. This card can also indicate someone making deeper inroads into a spiritual practice.

THE QUEEN OF WANDS – The queen is the passive recipient of the imagination's rewards. At this point, creativity is automatic. The artist can engage with his or her art, and a unique outcome is guaranteed. The black cat and the bright sunflower seem to indicate a person who can channel the positive and negative forces of creation.

THE KING WANDS – The king is the master of the element of fire. It burns within him at full force, but he can control it. He can conceive anything, and creativity is second nature to him. To **not** create would be difficult at this point. Among the kings, he has the most potential to create and destroy – only the King of Swords, through a rational organization, can possibly overcome him.

Chapter Four

How to Use Your Tarot Cards

<u>Conversing with The Tarot</u>

With a general understanding of the Major and Minor Arcana, you will be ready to work with the tarot. More than anything, it can offer you advice and help you view situations more clearly.

One way to consult the tarot is to use a **spread**. A spread is simply a way to lay out cards in specific positions. Based on a card's position in a spread, it will have a particular meaning. There are many, many spreads. Personally, I think there is an overemphasis on spreads in the tarot literature. It may be helpful to know what a card in a certain place means, but you can get the same information by simply asking better questions of the tarot. Because spreads can confuse beginners, I'm not going to use them in this book.

It is more important when getting started to grow comfortable with the cards themselves. Learn to assess your feelings about them. If this feels too free-form for you, remember that somebody **invented** every spread in use. Just as every religious orthodoxy and ceremony was once new, spreads are an arbitrary creation. You may adopt the traditions of others – this can be powerful – but it can be more liberating to create your own traditions. How you approach tarot reflects how you approach life. If you find you need a spread, they are easily found online and in books.

To begin getting advice from the cards, start with simple questions. When you put a question to the tarot, you are essentially questioning yourself and the larger Self that includes all of the universe. You can ask simple information questions (yes or no questions, for example), but better questions will yield better answers. So while you can ask questions like, Should, I buy this house? – the phrasing of that question raises a lot of problems. Should you buy this house according to **whom**? Should you buy it if you really want a secure place to live? Should you buy it if you want more freedom? The question supposes that you are a creature incapable of independent thought and need to be told what you **should** do.

But let's say you still want **advice** about buying a certain house. With that in mind, you can ask the question differently:

What outcome can I expect by buying this house?

Or

How happy will I be living in this house?

These types of questions go beyond a binary of yes and no. Every situation has its positive and negative aspects. By asking open-ended questions, you allow for more nuance in your tarot's answers.

Picking a card is once again, completely up to you. My method: shuffle the cards, clear my mind, and relax. I'll often close my eyes and ask my question to myself. Approach the tarot as you approach your highest self: with patience, gratitude, and reverence. I will often cut the deck and take the card I find. Sometimes I spread all of the cards out and slowly hover my hand over them. When it feels right, I take the card my finger is over.

If this all seems arbitrary and random, it may well be. But in choosing a card, the tarot seems to give you the card you need. The answer may seem wrong or even like a joke. It may seem like the exact opposite of an appropriate answer. When this happens, the tarot may be shining a spotlight on some aspect of a situation you're neglecting. Instead of giving you an answer you want, the tarot can steer you toward a necessary confrontation. Also, consider the frame of mind that needs a specific answer. **How** you converse with the tarot will teach you more than any specific answer.

As you shuffle your deck, sometimes a card will spontaneously fall out. I call this kind of card a jumper. Rather than put it back in the deck, I allow that this card so eagerly wanted to reveal itself that it jumped to my attention. Is it silly to anthropomorphize an inert card? Sure, but no more than

Using the tarot itself. If you accidentally come across an old friend while walking down the street, you give it meaning. It stirs up memories in the brain and steers you down a different road. You may have a completely different day because of that chance meeting. The cards you select in the tarot have the same activating principle. If you leave home ten minutes later than usual, you will have a completely different day. It may be similar in the grand scheme of things, but it will be different in details. And sometimes these details add up and send you into a totally different universe.

Once a card is chosen, take some time to study it. What kind of energy does it emote? Any work of art has energy. An action movie might get you excited. A gentle piece of classical music can help you get to sleep. It is virtually impossible to create a work of art without some kind of energy. Energy is its own brand of information. So consider the feeling you get from the card.

Also, consider what associations it brings. Journaling about a card can help you look deeper into what it's trying to tell you. Wherever your mind goes is where it needs to go. All the tarot does is stir up the necessary contents that are already inside you.

If, for example, I have some free time on Sunday, I might ask, What is the best way to spend Sunday? If the card that comes up is the Ace of Wands, it seems that some sort of creative or spiritual activity might be a good choice. I've been involved with writing and meditation groups, and I remember that I haven't done either in a while. That might be the best use of my time for Sunday. Obviously, the tarot isn't **telling** me what to do. But it shines a spotlight on my mind's contents.

Another example: I ask the tarot, Would now be a good time to get a dog? The card I pull from the deck is the 18th card of the Major Arcana, the Moon. The Moon card actually has a dog on it! But I look at that dog howling at the moon with the wolf, and I remember the wild energy a dog has. As fun as it would be to have a dog, it would be a lot of responsibility, and it would probably be better to wait a while longer. At least until I have more time and room for a dog. Once again, the tarot has not **told** me whether I should get a dog. It has only helped me see the situation more clearly.

In this way, the tarot can help you find a solution to any dilemma. In addition to journaling, here are some other ways to work with the tarot.

DO A DAILY READING

You can consult the tarot without having a specific question. In the morning, simply ask the tarot for a card appropriate for that day. I'll often ask for three cards. It's surprising how all three cards will work their way into my day.

USE A CARD AS YOUR PHONE OR DESKTOP BACKGROUND

I often ask the tarot for a necessary phone background for the month. This may be a lesson or mindset I will be working on. Having it on my phone guarantees, I will think about it throughout the month. Putting it on your computer as your desktop background also works.

MEDITATE ON AN IMAGE

You can sit comfortably, relax your mind, and take an image in. Turning off rational thought may be the best way to approach this exercise. It will allow you to connect to the card's energy and enter that state of being. You can do this with your eyes open and look at the card itself, or with your eyes closed, holding the image in your mind.

MAKE ART FROM THE CARDS

A card can inspire a work of art. You might do a painting or sculpture based on a card. It doesn't have to look anything like the original. It is ultimately about your mind, not the card. Similarly, you could write a story, poem, song, or something else based on the card. What scenario does the card suggest to you? If you are an actor, try to become the character on the card. Follow your intuition.

When you return to the card, you may find that its meaning has opened up for you.

START OR JOIN A TAROT GROUP

A tarot group lets you tap into the collective wisdom of others, and see things that would otherwise be impossible. Also, you'll be able to help others see through their tarot blind spots.

FIND TAROT CORRESPONDENCES

Can you connect the tarot to other things? Sure. Whether it's the Teenage Mutant Ninja Turtles, the Myers-Briggs personality types, the Beatles, or Harry Potter houses, there is no shortage of correspondences that can be made with the tarot. Doing this will allow you to see the larger patterns that the tarot indicates.

STUDY TAROT LITERATURE

Every book or video about the tarot can add to your collective knowledge. In addition to standard texts, fiction such as **Gravity's Rainbow**, **Illuminatus!** And the comic book **Promethea** were helpful for getting my head around the cards.

MAKE YOUR OWN TAROT DECK

The tarot should be as personal as possible. At the very least, make a conscious choice about the deck you use, finding one that resonates with you. But if you feel up to the challenge, make your own deck. This can be done with colored pencil on 3 x 5 cards, as paintings, digitally, or however, you choose.

Chapter Five

Card Combinations, Patterns and Elemental Dignities

As a proficient reader when you have two cards that come up in a reading that has a similar meaning, it's really quite subtle, so it's important to make sure that your customers or subjects really understand the message that's been given to them. There are several ways that you can end up finding patterns in reading. In this section, we'll focus on the most common examples of cards that often come up in a reading or the cards that are often paired so that you can see the patterns of how to read these card combinations and hopefully derived a much stronger message out of them that could be relevant to your subject.

Similar Meanings

The similarity of meanings and card combinations can be adjusted or change depending on which card it is paired with. Examples of cards that often come up and have a relatively similar meaning are the Seven of Pentacles and the Knight of Pentacles; the Eight of Swords and the Devil Card; Two of Cups and Five of Cups; Ten of Swords and Wheel of Fortune. Take note though that these cards can come with other pairs or come up more often, it can come in various ways, but it's almost as if these cards are carrying around the same energy with them.

The Seven of Pentacles and the Knight of Pentacles

The Seven of Pentacles have meaning associated with attention to detail, diligence, patience; sometimes it signifies delayed results or slow progress that could be happening in your subject's life. It can also mean that the person has not been really able to harvest or get results on whatever he/she is working on, so it generally means that the person could be working hard, putting a lot of effort and being patient in order to reap the rewards. Often times, this card is paired with Knight of Pentacles which has some sort of similar connotations, (of course if the Seven of Pentacles is paired with a different card, it will have a totally different meaning), the Knight of Pentacles or sometimes referred to as the Prince of Pentacles can often relate to stability, loyalty, being very practical, pragmatic and a card that associates with seeking security, does things slowly, someone who thinks about the kind of effort that he/she is willing to put into in order to achieve a certain growth or progress without rushing in.

So from all these meanings and associated adjectives, you can see that from the two cards, there are similarities of meanings – there's slowness, practicality, pragmatism, there's also steady of progress, and the theme of "not reaping the rewards immediately unless much effort is exerted." These will be the highlights when the two cards come up, so from those similar meanings, you can easily interpret that your subject might not be reaching fulfillment, completion or success at this point of their lives and that they may need to be patient because there will be a steady but slow progress that will be happening.

These meanings that you draw from the similar connotations of both cards can be related to your subject's career, relationship, dreams etc. Which means that they might need to be patient in their work or perhaps put in a lot of effort in their relationships; it could be reliable but steady not necessarily full of passion but perhaps practicality.

Now if the Seven of Pentacles is paired with a different card, say, for example, the Hanged Man, it can have a sort of similar meaning, but the focus of the message will most likely be different. The Hanged Man card is associated with words like surrender, pause, reflection, inaction, and standstill. It is still related to the meaning of the Seven of Pentacles because the theme is all about something that is not coming to fruition right away, but in this case, it could be less on the practicality or hard work. Perhaps, the focus of the message is that the rewards will definitely be delayed due to some kind of standstill along the way.

These meanings were derived simply because that's the strongest common denominator between the two cards, so as a tarot card reader that's what you should highlight more. These are some examples where parts of them have a similar meaning, which is why the message becomes very strong in the reading.

The Eight of Swords and the Devil Card

These cards again have similar meanings; the Eight of Swords is a card that is associated with self – limitation, it often means that the subject could be restricting themselves and not moving out of the situation even if he/she can. This card also means that there's a lack of clarity and vision or sort of self – entrapment because the subject may not know where he/she is going and have no idea how to get there.

The Devil Card, on the other hand, is associated with meanings like temptation, attachment to things, and entrapment, but it's more about dealing with one's 'inner demons' or inner imprisonment. It could also mean attaching oneself to something that is not healthy or good. So from the meaning of these two cards, you can focus on the part that they are binding themselves to a thought or belief system as well as to things or people that could be limiting your subject and not allowing them to be free. There's an attachment issue, self – entrapment or self – limitation.

Now, if you paired the Devil Card with the Seven of Cups, it can again have a similar meaning, but the focus of the message is different. As with the Seven of Cups, it's a card associated with imagination, visions, delusions, skewed perspective, and moving to things that are not in your best interest. Most of the time, this card represents substance abuse if the person is in a difficult situation, so if this card is paired with the Devil Card (with a meaning of attachment to things that aren't healthy), the message you can focus on is that your subject could be attaching or depending themselves on something like a substance, toxic relationships or something that is not healthy.

Two of Cups and Five of Cups

The Two of Cups is about making a connection with others and building a bond with people. The Five of Cups, on the other hand, is also about a person's emotional life, intuition, feelings and relationships with others, how a person reconciles things, and about the inner world. So if you encounter pulling out two or more cups in a reading, that means that your subject is dealing with some kind of emotional part of themselves or relationship situations. In this case, you can interpret it as something that's been a loss (probably due to a breakup or death of a loved one) and your subject may need to be positive about it. So if it's a relationship issue, it means that your subject should look at the positive side of it even if it could be something of a breakup, you could advise him/her to let go or move on.

If the Two of Cups is paired with a Three of Cups, there's still a cup theme (or a relationship theme), but it's with more than one person like friendships, family, etc. It represents your communication with others or positive connection with people. So if these two cards are paired, you can interpret it in a way where there's the emotional situation going on but it's on a positive level, and it's more than one person. The point is you're looking for a pattern, but each cup has a different meaning or has your subject is focusing on a different area at the moment.

Ten of Swords and Wheel of Fortune

The number ten usually means that you're nearing the end of the cycle or you're at the end of the cycle, so that could mean that the person has gone through a lot or have experienced a lot of things already. The number ten is the closing of a cycle; the swords represent some challenges that a person has been through. So the Ten of Swords card has come to a point where a person is in a collapse kind of situation. However, it's also saying that a new cycle is about to begin, so the person has to take a look at how you can prepare for that next cycle.

The Ten of Swords is connected to the Wheel of Fortune because the Wheel of Fortune card represents a cyclical nature of things, so that means that a person goes through phases and move from one to another, there's always a change or flux, and it also talks about the "seasons of life." These card combinations can mean that your subject is at the end of that particular situation or even in their life – that they're probably about to close that "chapter" but a new one is coming.

Elemental Dignities

Essentially elemental dignities will make you determine if the card is well – dignified or ill – dignified. It also depends on what another card combination is next to it. You'll learn if a card combination has an element that speaks the same language or the opposite language. Elemental dignities basically pertain to the relationships of each element to one another.

Qualities of Elements

Before determining the relationship of each element, you must first know the qualities or characteristics of the elements in a card. Just like in any other field, particularly subjects that deal with nature or energy fields, the elements are composed of Air, Fire, Water, and Earth. In Tarot cards, the air element is represented by swords, the water element is represented by cups, the Earth element is pentacles, and the fire is represented by wands. The four elements relate to the four kinds found in the tarot deck. By looking at the four elements, a reader can determine some of its characteristics.

There's also the concept of polarity in the four elements which is also divided by two; the first pair is Fire (Wands) and Air (Swords) which are also called active elements; the second pair is Water (Cups) and Earth (Pentacles) which are also called passive elements. The former paired elements are masculine, and the latter pair is feminine.

Masculine elements are active, outgoing, extroverted, and have a "yang energy." It can also be described as direct, assertive, sustaining, autonomous, and often times self – motivated. These masculine elements also focus on the self, and its 'powers' come from within oneself. On the other hand, the feminine elements have characteristics that are receptive, indirect, passive, introverted, soft, intuitive, nurturing and it has a tendency to look outside of oneself especially for advice or verifications.

Elemental Dignities and its Relationships

Now that you've learned what the elements are and their representation in the tarot deck, the next important thing to know is how these elements relate to one another. As a reader, you're going to encounter combinations that come up in readings so you have to know its meaning and relationships because it can also affect the message of the cards.

The fire element is usually opposite the water, which makes sense because water can put out a fire, so having these elements means that they weaken one another. Once these elements show up in a reading, you can easily determine that those opposing energies are weakening one another and there's also a flux between these two characteristics or aspects of life that are showing up. Another elemental pairs that weaken each other is air and earth because the air is above and the earth is below.

Cards of the same element like fire (wands) and air (swords) which are also masculine strengthen each other. On the other hand, feminine elements like water (cups) and earth (pentacles) also speak the same language, which therefore strengthens each other as well. Elements that neutralized each other are fire to earth as well as air to water. These things could be quite hard to remember, but what you can do is to give them acronyms or have your own method of memorizing these concepts so you can easily relate it during your readings.

So basically when a card is 'elementally well dignified' that means it is being strengthened by the card next to it, on the other hand, if a card is 'elementally ill dignified' it is being weakened by the card beside it. So if for example, a card shows up and it's a sword, and then it is next to another sword then it is at its strongest point because it can express its full potential and therefore elementally well dignified. If a card is in the same suit, it's going to speak the same language and vice – versa. So if you pulled a sword (air) and the card next to it is a pentacle (earth), it weakens one another, and therefore it is elementally ill dignified.

Well – Dignified (Strong Position) Cards

In this section, you'll learn some examples of what it means to have a well – dignified cards. These cards have similar polarity (either masculine or feminine) elemental energy to it. We'll take a look at the Three of Wands and King of Wands; Three of Wands and King of Swords for the well – dignified cards and the Eight of Pentacles and Knight of Swords for the ill – dignified examples.

Three of Wands and King of Wands

As what you've learned, wand cards are equal to the fire element and therefore has a masculine energy that is well dignified. These cards have similar characteristics; it is active, outgoing, and has clarity in the decision – making the process. So once these two cards are pulled, it can mean that your subject has a significant amount of masculine energy and that he/she is not going to have difficulty in terms of focus or being direct. They will pretty much force themselves to make something happen to accomplish a particular goal; they could also be assertive and self – motivated. So studying the elemental aspect of the cards can make a reader say not just the meaning of the cards or literal interpretation of it but also be able to recognize the polarity of the elements it represents.

As you can see the card is well dignified and therefore is at its highest expression if you look at it this way.

Three of Wands and King of Swords

As what you've learned earlier wands are represented by fire and swords are represented by air, which is another masculine energy. It may not be quite well – dignified compared to Three of Wands card and the King of Wands card (since it's basically of the same element) but it's still well positioned because they're speaking the same language – the more outgoing masculine language and because fire strengthens air and vice – versa. So if the King of Swords is paired with the Three of Wands your subject may have created something to a certain point but at this point must make certain logical decisions or really analyze something to create a sound decision going forward.

Four of Cups and Four of Pentacles

Cups (water) and Pentacles (earth) are both feminine polarity. They share characteristics that are receptive, passive, introverted, and have a tendency to look on the outside to figure out what to do. Since they are both feminine, they are well-dignified cards and the fact that their numbers are the same means that they also speak the same language, so it has a lot of similarities to it however, this is where you have too much passive energy and potentially too little progress wherein a person could feel as if they're being controlled by other things or being in a passive position.

The number four signifies stability, but it can also mean that there could be intrinsic limitations that prevent an individual from growing or achieving something. If you pulled out a bunch of feminine energy and the number four, then there's a lot of passivity or stagnation or maybe that individual is stuck in a certain position and that the only way is to take a risk to be able to get out of that restriction to be able to learn. You can also advise your subject to get in touch with more masculine energy in order to help them to move forward or get out of their own "box." On the other hand, if you pulled out cards and saw a lot of active masculine energy it could mean that there's conflict, fight or competition, the solution is to get in touch with the female elements or passive principles.

Ill – Dignified (Weak Position) Card

The examples in this section will focus on cards that are opposite each other or weakened by the card next to it.

Eight of Pentacles and Knight of Swords

The Eight of Pentacles is an earth element, and the Knight of Swords is an air element which means they are opposite and therefore weakening each other and not speaking the same language. The Knight of Swords card has a masculine polarity to it since it is an air element; it has characteristics of being action-oriented, outgoing, adventurous, flexible, and pretty much has masculine energy to it. Pentacles, in general, are all about manifestations in the physical realm, it has tendencies to move slower and only working on things that are tangible and kind of earthbound. When it comes to the Eight of Pentacles represent someone who diligently works, takes time to develop a skill and someone who is working very hard over a long period of time.

So if you think about it, the Eight of Pentacles is all about taking one's time to create something while the Knight of Swords focuses on direct action and just going after whatever idea comes to mind. These characteristics are opposing and doesn't go very well together, if your subject pulled this card combination, it could mean that they are in a flux between these two opposing energies so most likely these energies are fighting against one another or perhaps your subject needs to be aware it because it's not going to help them in moving forward.

Your subject may also need some sort of compromise to these two opposing elements in order to bring things in harmony or balance. It could also mean that the Eight of Pentacles need to accept the brilliant ideas of the Knight of Swords, and the Knight of Swords should need to slow down and take time to think things out. So you need to let your subject know that they have opposing energies that they need to be aware of and work out.

Chapter Six
Card Placements within a Tarot Spread

In this section, you'll learn some of the ways in which a card is strengthened or weakened depending on the placement within a reading; it can be related to an elemental dignity or other meanings. Knowing the card placement or even card reversal within a tarot spread can affect your reading as well. I'm going to give you some examples of how card placement may have an impact on the meaning of the card and how it is strengthened or weakened by being in a particular position.

Cards That Fall in an Outcome/Final/Future Position

Many different spreads have some type of outcome or final position, so if you have that kind of spread for your subject, you'll know that those cards are in a very strong position because it's showing you a final outcome or a point of completion.

- **Six of Wands** - Six of Wands, six is a number that represents a certain level of completion; it's also a card that celebrates victory in a positive way.

- **Ten of Pentacles** - Ten of Pentacles is another great card in the outcome position, if you have a ten that shows up even in other types of cards, it usually signifies a final point in some type of cycle, as for

Ten of Pentacles, it's a positive outcome for some kind of success in career, relationships, family or other areas. If the ten is in the Swords card or Wands, it could be quite a challenging end or one that has been through strife compared to cups and pentacles. But again, seeing a ten is great because it means that the cycle is in a final point and a new cycle is coming.

- **The World** - The World card in itself is already showing an outcome or completion as well; it also means putting an effort over a period of time and seeing success on a physical level. It can also have a spiritual connotation, and it's a well-dignified card because it's in a very strong position.

- **The Sun** - The Sun card in a final position means a positive outlook; it also shows confidence and just a naturally strong card to have for the outcome.

- **The Ten of Cups** - Ten of Cups shows happiness, connections with loved ones, abundance, and a lot of great things have happened for an individual. It also signifies an emotional satisfaction.

- **The Wheel of Fortune** - The Wheel of Fortune again shows a level of completion in phases or cycles. You can assume that one cycle is ending and another one will begin soon. This card also holds a strong position in the outcome reading.

Cards that Fall in a Challenge or Obstacle Position

Cards that are in positive positions aren't the only cards that are strengthened because what we're talking about here in this chapter is whether a card is well dignified in the sense of its meaning. The card must be in its purest meaning when it comes up, so cards that are challenging or difficult in reading must be something that your client or subject might need to overcome.

- **Three of Swords** – is a card that shows separation, difficulty, and denotes some kind of pain or anger that has been caused by difficult relationships that can be felt at a very deep level. So if this card comes up in a challenge position, it's about how your subject can overcome the pain and difficulty that he/she has experienced and how to deal with it.

- **The Devil Card** – the devil card denotes some form of attachment mentally or physically that might be holding your subject back from being whoever he/she wants to be or do.

- **Five of Cups** – this card denotes that one should overcome some sort of grief or despair that he/she sometimes feel and go through. Your subject should learn how to deal with those emotions as best as they can to move forward.

- **Nine of Swords** - this card in a challenge position denotes that one should overcome personal anxieties or difficulties. Your subject should believe in his/herself and not over - analyzed everything mentally.

Reading Cards in Tarot Spread Position

In this section, you'll learn how to read a negative card in a positive placement or vice – versa. Tarot cards, in general looks at the scope of a human's life or an individual's psyche and how we live our lives. Every card in the tarot conveys some kind of lesson that you can learn from whether it's in a positive or negative position. You need to understand that nothing is black and white – which means that nothing is completely positive or negative; there are always two sides to it and a lesson to learn from.

Positive Cards in a Negative Placement vs. Negative Cards in a Positive Placement

This concept can be very hard to grasp especially if you're a beginner it's because most newbie readers read cards in its literal form or the meaning of it, but if the card is placed in a contradicting situation, it can be hard to analyze and draw meaning from. As with most expert tarot card readers, they have developed their own reading system in reading cards that are either in a negative or positive placement but their common denominator or perhaps the guiding principle is that tarot cards are not one dimensional, even if it's a positive cards there'll still be some negative aspect to it, same with negative cards. Some readers refer to it as a shadow, warning, or edge if a card has positive meaning but is placed in a negative position or vice – versa. If you understand the edge or shadows of a card, you'll be able to understand how to read them in any kind of placement. Here are some examples:

- **The Sun Card**

The Sun card is a positive card, so if it lands in an outcome or final position within a spread, then you can automatically say that it will be about optimism, happiness, fulfillment or a person has shone in its own way in life because that's the usual denotation of that card. Now, if the Sun Card comes up in a negative position, it may denote that your subject may not be living life to the fullest, they may not be acknowledging the joys in their life, your client may not be fully expressing who they are or who they want to be or what if your client does not feel free to express something or may not have the freedom to live life on their own terms. Those are the ideas that you could ask or share to your client if a positive card like this comes up in a negative position.

- **Three of Swords**

The Three of Swords card is a difficult card or a negative card because it usually denotes pain, separation, betrayal, isolation, heartbreak, and suffering. So if this card comes up in a positive placement, the edge or shadow of this card could be a call for healing. The lesson or the message you can convey to your client is to determine how one can start the healing process or identify and acknowledge those sufferings so that they'll be able to start healing in that particular area of their life. If your client is asking for advice and this card comes up, then you can tell him/her to face the pain they are feeling and possibly do something with what could help them heal a particular feeling or angst they may have.

- **The Emperor Card**

The Emperor card is all about structure, order, formation so it can be related to rules and regulations. It also has some kind of authority or leadership quality to it. It's a positive card that could be great if pulled in an outcome position because it can mean that one is becoming a leader or perhaps one needs to pay attention to a structure to maintain an orderly kind of environment. But if this card is in a negative position, it can mean that the power or control brought about by leadership can be too much to handle. It can mean that an individual is overpowering or over - controlling a situation; there are probably too many rules, laws or regulations that can be a hindrance to freedom or creativity; it can also mean that a person is too limited in his/her approach and he/she may need to let go of some of these limiting beliefs. So if this card is in a negative placement, it will focus on how much control or power is happening as well as how the structure may limit freedom to a person or to other people.

- **Nine of Swords**

The Nine of Swords is a negative card that's all about anxiety, mental anguish, depression and some sort of feedback loop where a person is constantly thinking about something that's painful or obsessing about something that is bothering him/her for a long time. It could also bring up a level of being ill due to a stressful situation. There's a lot of strife and isolation for this card but if the Nine of Swords comes up in a positive position, the advice you can give to your subject to overcome a situation is to maybe be able to step back and figure out what it is that's causing them these anxieties so they can find a way to solve it, kind of getting to the root cause of the problem. Another meaning you can derive from this card in a positive way is again healing, so perhaps this card is telling your subject to take time to heal and just let it all out, let all the tears flow so that he/she can be cleanse inside out and be able to let go of all the things that is troubling them and move past this difficulty.

- **Nine of Cups**

The Nine of Cups denotes that one hasn't reached the end yet, but they're almost there. It's a positive card that represents one's emotional self or inner world, relationship with oneself or with others, creativity and the likes (remember it's a feminine polarity). It also means that a person has reached a certain level of abundance or fulfillment, but they are alone. So the edge of this card, if it's placed in a negative position, is that the person is "alone," meaning that the individual may not be connecting or sharing what they have accomplished with other people. You can also consider a level of complacency as well as overindulgence in the individual's part.

- **The Five of Cups**

The Five of Cups has an intrinsic edge to it; as you now know, the cups talks all about relationships, emotions, inner world, creativity, and intuition. This card, in particular, denotes loss, grief, emotional pain, and difficult to let go so this is in itself a negative card. So the edge of the card, when it is placed in a positive position, is that there's some kind of hope after all this pain and strife, and it means that an individual needs to let go of whatever he/she lose in order to move on to see the positive things that are still there.

Three Card Spreads

Three card spreads are usually used to see what's coming up for the next three months or possibly the kind of events that will unfold with regards to the subject's physical, mental or even emotional aspect. What you can do is to let your client choose one card for each of the next three months for them to have a glimpse of the future. If you're doing to a three card spread what you can do is to assign the first card that is picked for the next month (not the month you are in), and then the next card is for the consecutive month and so on. In this section, we'll give you some examples of how to read cards that could mean the next three months for your subject.

Example #1: The Four of Cups, Ace of Wands, Four of Wands

This is where the other lessons will come in, so if you remember the principle of elemental dignities you can use that in initially reading the cards and incorporate other tarot reading principles from there.

From this set of example, you'll notice that Wands card are predominant since there are two out of three. The predominance of wands or the fire element energy is going to be important for the next three months. It could mean that an individual may develop some type of interest or passion in some endeavor or a certain drive and energy. They might also use a more masculine polarity, which means that they'll probably be more action-oriented in order to achieve something. They'll also probably start off the next three months with the cup energy, which means that there could be an emotional element involved.

You can also take a look at another aspect, which is the numbers of the cards. So from this example, there are a four of cups and four of wands the number four signifies structure, order, stability, limitation, and there's possibly a manifestation in the physical world. So you can look at it in the way of the flow of events, will there be a stagnation in the next three months or what kind of progress is going to happen, is it from stagnation to action or vice – versa, etc. So from this example, the four of cups (the first month) denotes stagnation, the ace of wands denotes not much action; the four of wands denotes a significant form of action, so that could be the possible flow in the next three months.

The advice you can give to your client is that in the first month (four of cups) they may want to determine what's stopping them from doing something or focus on the possible opportunities around them. You can also suggest feeling their emotions about certain things but not get stuck with it and recognize that the difficulty they are feeling at the moment is temporary.

For the next month, the ace of Wands suggests that you have to figure out how to maximize that opportunity because you'll experience a spark of inspiration, passion, enthusiasm or an idea, you'll have the energy in doing something not just in career-related things but other aspects as well. So this is the month to actually start doing something and taking that first step towards a particular interest.

The third card (four of wands) suggests that by the third month, your subject may have already manifest something from that spark of interest, it also suggests that an individual has prospered from it or made it stable, in short, there'll be some type of success involve or a positive outcome in career, relationship or other aspects.

Example #2: The World, Four of Cups, Six of Wands

Again, you'll have to look at the flow of the cards, so you can check out if there are similarities or none at all, the numbers, the cards, and the overall flow. If there's no repeating aspect to the cards just like this example, it doesn't necessarily mean that there's no pattern – it's just not that obvious. So you have to go back to finding the flow of events for the cards and what they could possibly mean.

For this set, the example will be a query about relationships. The first card pulled for the first month is The World card, the second is the Four of Cups, and the third is the Six of Wands – so if you think about it the pattern is like an up and down sort of thing which can apply to the status of your subject's relationship in the next three months. The relationship starts at the top (The World Card), then it goes downhill (Four of Cups) and climbs up again (Six of Wands). So overall, you can assume that there were aspects of the relationship that's fulfilling as represented by the world card and maybe that relationship became grounded or serious, then at some point they could experience some sort of challenge that pertains to emotions which is represented by the four of cups, your subject may be undergoing some sort of unhappiness in a particular aspect of their relationship, and they may need to figure out what's really going on or perhaps what's causing that feeling of discontentment in order to overcome that downhill flow.

The six of wands represent some success, triumph, and optimism since the number six also means a sense of balance and harmony. It can mean that the relationship has overcome whatever emotional challenge or difficulty that they have experience.

Example #3: Situation Cards, Obstacle Cards, Outcome Cards

In this example, we'll use The Hanged Man, The Lovers, and The Chariot. Now, these cards are all in the Major Arcana, so it means that a situation is of major importance or significant for the individual's spiritual or psychological level. It's not about the physical surroundings or daily life (minor arcana), it's going to represent something that is much profound than that.

- **Situation Card: The Hanged Man**

The Hanged Man is all about the spiritual state or the unconscious state. This card is not about dealing with daily life; it's more of connecting to oneself or on a spiritual level. So if you pulled this card for a situation placement, it could mean that an individual is contemplating, it can also mean a difficult time because the person is not necessarily moving forward or the situation is at a standstill or suspension. This card suggests a period of reflection or that a person should look at things from a different perspective. Your subject may also spiritually need to connect, but he/she is not connecting to a certain thing.

- **Challenge Card: The Lovers**

The Lovers card is associated with passion or spiritually love, where a person connects with someone or something that has a great depth or spiritual meaning. So if you pulled this card for a challenging placement, it could mean that it's related to choices that one needs to make or the crossroads that a person is currently on. The obstacle that is represented by this card is that a person may be lacking clarity or that one must make decisions to move forward.

- **Outcome Card: The Chariot**

The Chariot card is associated with success, triumph, or having control over a situation in order to take oneself to a certain place or goal. This card represents decision making and also pertains to the freedom to use one's will or power to do certain tasks.

So the flow for this set of cards is that an individual is moving from a lack of clarity and not knowing which way to go as represented by the Hanged Man, then making decisions (The Lovers) and finally having that internal will and drive to put something into play to make a progression and move forward as represented by The Chariot card.

Chapter Seven
Card Reversals and Timing

There are various theories about how readers can interpret the meaning of a reversed card, in this section though we'll only brush up on some common meanings of reversed cards. If your client is asking what he/she needs to learn or the challenge that needs to be overcome the reversed cards are in a very strong position because it can show the avenue that your subject can address or change. The timing in tarot cards deals with how your subject should approach a situation, or the kind of timing is on the current reading. The timing will show you how something is going to unfold or what your subject needs to know in terms of going to the next step.

Card Reversals

We'll provide some examples of how you can interpret the meaning of the card when it is drawn or pulled out in a reverse position. Basically, you just have to sort of reverse its meaning or put it in another perspective.

- **Eight of Swords** – this card generally means that a circumstance or perception bind someone and that a person needs to recognize that they can overcome that, so if this card is reversed, it can signify that an individual is breaking through some of the constraints that are imposed upon a person or perhaps oneself. It can also mean freeing oneself from some kind of limiting factors.

- **The Devil Card** – as mentioned previously, it can mean attachment from certain things that aren't healthy or at a person's best interest. So if it's reverse, it can mean that an individual is in a more growing awareness or in a state where an individual wants to be free of a particular attachment.

- **Eight of Wands** – if this card is reverse, it can have issues in terms of moving forward because there could be some issues, delays, or even difficulties.

- **Six of Swords** – once this card is reversed, it could also mean that there'll be delays in moving through a certain situation or leaving the past behind either physically or mentally.

Timing in Tarot Cards

Sometimes in a reading, you may have to deal with what kind of approach your client should do. If you have a reading where your subjects or clients are asking advice on a particular situation they are in, the following examples will show you how to recognize some cards in the tarot deck.

Seven of Pentacles and Knight of Pentacles

Seven of Pentacles is all about having diligence and patience to work hard on something but not being able to reap the rewards right away. So it's a card that will tell you and your subject that something in their life may not be coming into fruition at the moment or any time soon. Knight of Pentacles similarly is a card that denotes stagnation. The Knight of Pentacles does things slowly and is quite methodical compared to the Knight of Swords or Knight of Wands; he will not rush into doing things but if he decides to do things he will do it well and will take his time in doing it.

If these kinds of cards come up, the timing will be slower, probably more methodical, it's something that's going to happen over a period of time, and your client may not necessarily see the rewards of whatever he/she is doing right away, and patience may be required.

The Hanged Man and Four of Swords

Both of these cards denote that quick action and activity is not going to happen. The Hanged Man card can mean that your subject may need to pause or reflect. It can also mean that your subject may not have the energy to do a particular endeavor at this time. It can also mean not being able to move forward and that an individual may need to surrender something to move forward. The Four of Swords is about a period of recuperation, and it mainly denotes a healing phase probably from stress or a broken relationship. So these cards can tell your subject that things may not be moving forward at this time in terms of unfolding events.

The Knight of Swords and Eight of Wands

The Eight of Wands is a card that is looking forward to something; it has some positive element to it and usually denotes a fast pace of progress or being able to move forward. It has a lot of quick energy in it, and some information can also come to you, which will help you accomplish things faster. Knight of Swords is a similarly active card, so if your client asks you how something is going to unfold or the timing of a certain event, once you pull these cards it can mean that something is going to happen very quickly, but of course, there's also some precaution because you might also need to take a step back and not rush too much.

Cards Denoting Transition or New Beginnings

Cards that show transition or change can also be found in the Major Arcana and the minor ones, in this section, you'll learn some of these cards and how they suggest a change or new beginnings in an individual's life.

- **The Death Card** – this card notoriously means that an individual is going through some kind of change and because of that transition; the person will be changed, moved through it and possibly come out a different person either growing or developing in some way.

- **The Tower of Card** – it denotes an abrupt change and may mean that an individual may sometimes need to let go of whatever we are holding to allow a significant change to occur.

- **The Fool Card** – denotes that an individual may need to take a leap of faith, start something fresh or doing something that you haven't done before is required.
- **Six of Swords** – denotes that you need to move through a situation because a better one is ahead. It can also mean that an individual may need to move to a new location or travel for a change.

For transition cards, your subject may need to recognize that a new start, a new learning or a new approach is required, these things are important in readings that has a position around that particular theme.

Relationship Cards

If you're going to do a reading on relationships, there are a lot of cards in the tarot deck that speaks clearly about relationships. Regardless if a card has a positive connotation or it shows a negative spin or some sort of difficulty as long as it's in the realm of relationships, these cards will have a strong position in a reading.

- **Seven of Cups** – this card in terms of the relationship suggests that there are lots of emotions or desire but an individual may have lots of choices and might not be clear of how they feel or who to choose. It also denotes not having clarity in a relationship.

- **Knight of Cups** – this card can mean the style of a particular relationship and tends to be in a romantic placement.
- **Ten of Cups** – it denotes positivity, a sense of completion and happiness in a certain relationship.
- **The Knight of Pentacles** – it is a very practical earth card that denotes an individual has worked very hard, and in terms of relationship one or both parties are independent and self – sufficient. One or both parties may not want the kind of relationship that is being too dependent on one another.
- **Five of Swords** – the number five is denoting strife which can signify difficulties in a relationship. It can also mean a lot of competition or struggle.

Chapter Eight

The Meaning of Each Tarot Card

In this chapter, you'll learn the basic meanings of the tarot cards. You don't really need to memorize every meaning or interpretation of each card right away, but you have to know at least its background or the values, ideas, and principles it represents so that you can understand how it could relate to another card or to an aspect of one's life. You'll also get to learn the general meaning of the 'types' of cards found in the deck – they are called the Major Arcana and the Minor Arcana as well as what each suit (Wands, Swords, Pentacles, and Cups) represent.

You may notice that some cards have almost the same meaning or is somewhat related to one another, but as you learn more in the next chapters, you'll soon find out how the message of each card within each suit and its positions could tell a different story or may be interpreted from a different perspective.

The Major and Minor Arcana

THE MAJOR ARCANA

THE FOOL (0)

- A new phase of life begins
- The discovery of talents

- New Experiences
- Risk must be taken
- There's a need to abandon the old and start something
- Personal growth
- New development

THE MAGICIAN (1)

- Possibilities in a person
- New skills are available
- Potential is growing
- Opportunities and adventures unfolding
- Success in everything if a person utilizes his/her skills and talents

THE EMPRESS (2)

- Known as the mother of fertility and growth
- New things about to enter a situation
- There may be a birth coming or a new path in life
- Focuses on marriage, relationship, pregnancy, patience and motherhood

THE EMPEROR (3)

- A need to make something solid or to solidify something
- Focuses on building an idea or something with a firm structure

- Have values of authority, control, and dominance.
- Man of power
- An employer or an authority

THE HIGH PRIESTESS (4)

- A time for reflection
- Allows secrets to be revealed
- Shows potential abundance
- Urges people to pay attention to your dreams and intuition
- This card is all about truly understanding life's possibilities

THE HIEROPHANT (5)

- There's a need for spiritual purpose
- Talks about the search for a personal philosophy
- Encourages a person to increase studying and learning
- Focuses on humility and teachings
- Makes a person get through deeply frightening and hard situations
- This card can sometimes suggest marriage or a serious turn towards religion

THE LOVERS (6)

- A love affair with a trial or choice attached

- This card indicates that these decisions or choices are incredibly important and significant
- One must choose the right path
- A sign of true partnership
- It focuses in choosing intuitively rather than by the use of intellect

THE CHARIOT (7)

- Conflict within
- Struggles and battles
- Potential for victory
- Resolution of fights
- Moving forward
- Overcoming opposition through confidence
- Control and Determination
- It can also mean a journey or change of location

JUSTICE (8)

- Need for clarity of mind
- Impartial judgment
- Requires a balanced intellect
- Legal matters needing attention
- Calls for the fairest decision
- A person is also being called to account for one's actions and will be judged accordingly

THE TEMPERANCE (9)

- Harmony within relationships
- Suggests happy marriage or partnership
- Adaptation and coordination
- Balance
- Patience
- Moderation

THE STRENGTH (10)

- Suggests a person must face the things or the truth in a situation that you have been putting off for too long.
- Overcoming one's fears or doubts
- Courage
- Inner Will
- Optimism

THE HERMIT (11)

- Time for withdrawal
- Promotes silent meditation and solitude
- Patience is needed to confront one's inner world
- Could be someone who likes to or needs to work alone

THE WHEEL OF FORTUNE (12)

- Change in fortune

- New beginnings
- Suggests new chapter in life
- The Wheel makes a new turn
- Remain optimistic
- Someone who has faith that the Universe will take care of the situation

THE HANGED MAN (13)

- A sacrifice must be made to gain something of greater value
- Talks about waiting in order to allow new possibilities to arise
- Vulnerability
- Selflessness
- New Perspectives
- Suggests a willingness to adapt to changing circumstances

DEATH (14)

- Known as the most misunderstood card in the deck
- The end of something which has been lived out
- Suggests transformation or new beginnings will follow
- This card indicates a time of significant change and transition

THE DEVIL (15)

- A confrontation with the inner world
- Facing fears and inhibitions can foster growth
- The Devil reflects actual addictions and dependencies in one's life like alcohol, illegal drugs, toxic relationships, gambling, overspending
- Also, suggest breaking of bad or unhealthy habits or vices

THE TOWER (16)

- Focuses on breaking down existing forms
- Changing false structures and finding true values
- Change around the home
- Emotionally challenging periods in a person's life
- A time of great upheaval
- It symbolizes conflict and overall disruption, but it's for the greater good

THE STAR (17)

- It's about facing things you have been reluctant to deal with
- It could lead to good or bad things, but this action needs to be done

THE MOON (18)

- Fluctuation
- Uncertainty
- Confusion

- Passive
- Suggests of letting go of one's conscious mental blocks
- Encourages a person to allow his/her intuition to guide him/her

THE SUN (19)

- Optimism
- Passive
- Energetic or Vitality
- Abundance
- A time of clear vision
- It is about embracing your destiny and giving it everything you have got.
- Suggests happiness, triumph and good health
- Also relates to achievement
- Sometimes talks about traveling to a warm or tropical climate

JUDGEMENT (20)

- It's a time for reaping the rewards for past actions and reaching conclusions
- Suggests that a person may have assessed and evaluated his/her past experiences and have learned from them
- Rebirth or renewal

- Changes for the better
- Getting well after a long sickness
- Also suggests finding a new career or spiritual path

THE WORLD (21)

- Success
- Achievement
- Attainment
- The realization of a goal or the completion of a cycle
- Can also indicate world travel
- Suggests a feeling of being welcome anywhere you go

THE MINOR ARCANA

WANDS SUIT– wands is related to one's imagination and creativity; it is associated with the element of fire. It also focuses on action and movement and has risk-taking qualities to it as well as confidence, inward passion, and enthusasm.

Court Cards:

PAGE OF WANDS

- Serves as the instigator
- Curious and restless
- Suggests a creative Spark

KNIGHT OF WANDS

- Adventurer
- Has a youthful enthusiasm
- Has an appetite for risks
- Someone who is in search of challenge and excitement

QUEEN OF WANDS

- Usually motivated and dynamic
- Someone who knows how to multi-task
- She's a heroine and charming but can also be selfish at times

KING OF WANDS

- Has a forceful personality
- Visionary
- Willful
- Reckless
- Extremely creative and inventive
- Sometimes it can also mean that he's not paying attention to details

Pip Cards:

ACE OF WANDS (1)

- Has a lot of creative energy, drive, and vitality
- Has potential for success
- Initiative

- Boundless Energy
- Creative Power and Inspiration

TWO OF WANDS

- Suggests a more intuitive choice
- Two possibilities or duality
- Suggests equally good
- Firm plans should be done
- Envisioning the future
- Readiness for change
- Suggests that a person is standing in his past and future

THREE OF WANDS

- Suggests a stage of initial completion of a creative project
- Ideas are forming
- There are forces of new energy that is being generated
- Readiness to embark on a new adventure
- Taking opportunities
- Can also be about travelling

FOUR OF WANDS

- A time to pause for celebration after hard efforts
- Also suggests that a person should take a break, have a period of rest and learn to relax

- Sometimes it's known as the marriage card
- Harmony in one's home
- Aesthetic pleasures
- Positive connections

FIVE OF WANDS

- A time of struggle
- Challenges will constantly appear
- Expect difficulties ahead
- Open conflict
- Certain issues cause a lot of tension and confusion
- Lacking focus
- Suggests inner conflict or general chaos
- Can also mean that an individual is being pulled in different directions

SIX OF WANDS

- Public recognition
- Promotion
- Recognition for one's work
- Suggest success in any chosen field
- Supportive community

SEVEN OF WANDS

- Stiff competition must now be faced
- A person should hold one's ground

- Renewed determination
- Courage is necessary
- Suggests inner or outer battles
- It can also mean that an individual is prepared for a fight

EIGHT OF WANDS

- It's a card of ease; everything is happening at a fast pace
- There's a real sense of harmony
- Swiftness
- It's a period of fruitful progress after a delay or struggle
- Suggests that everything is in a person's favor but needs to continue pushing forward

NINE OF WANDS

- Strength in reserve can provide enough energy to win the battle
- The energy of a person seems exhausted, but it suggests that one should still move forward to reach completion
- Requires perseverance
- Acknowledges weariness before a resolution can occur

TEN OF WANDS

- There could be a danger implied in taking on more than one can cope with
- Inadequate awareness of one's limitations
- Can also mean that passion can be renewed since a new cycle is coming
- It means a release from the struggle

CUPS SUIT – The cups card is the suit that is related to the element of water. It relates to the inner realm not just pertaining to a person's emotions, but also one's unconscious mind, dreams, and intuition. It can also relate to relationships but in a deeper way.

Court Cards:

PAGE OF CUPS

- Vulnerable
- Introspection
- Emotional Sensitivity

KNIGHT OF CUPS

- Dreamer
- Soft-spoken
- Easy going and gentle
- Sincere

QUEEN OF CUPS

- Emotionally intense
- Can be intuitive and determined

- Can also be jealous and ruthless

KING OF CUPS

- Has a strong and controlling force
- Resists change in an emotional status quo
- One who likes to maintain power especially in relationships

Pip Cards:

ACE OF CUPS (1)

- High feelings and emotion
- New relationships
- Love affair
- The birth of a child
- Self – acceptance
- Spiritual guidance
- Gratitude and compassion

TWO OF CUPS

- Commitment to romance
- Partnership or friendship
- Emotional balance
- There's an attraction of two things or people even if it comes from different natures

THREE OF CUPS

- Suggest a celebration

- A time for rejoicing
- The commitment to a future project or endeavor has been made
- Suggests social life and successful partnerships/groups even from different natures
- Compatibility

FOUR OF CUPS

- Usually, the person is self-absorbed
- An individual is a content with the way things are
- Stability and confinement in terms of emotion
- There's an emotional uncertainty or self – doubt
- Someone who is not sure if they want to make a change
- Inability to make decisions
- Emotionally stuck

FIVE OF CUPS

- Regret over past actions
- Loss or betrayal in love
- Separation
- All is not lost even though it suggests loss
- Suggests that one should recognize what has been lost

SIX OF CUPS

- Past effort may bring present rewards

- Can also mean that an old lover may appear again
- Sentimental time
- Also known as a sibling card
- Mutual enjoyment in partnership

SEVEN OF CUPS

- Focuses on several choices available
- Careful decisions must be made
- Action
- There is a risk of illusion
- You need to avoid escapism protect yourself against unclear thinking
- Also suggests a search for wisdom or oneself
- Emotional confusion
- Self – doubt and can also be about the projection of problems into the outer world and how one should take responsibility for it

EIGHT OF CUPS

- Can mean that a person must leave the past behind
- Letting go of something even if it required much effort
- Suggests of walking away
- Encourages a person to pursue one's dream or ambitions
- Change of relationship status

- Emotional detachment
- Has willingness to walk into the unknown

NINE OF CUPS

- A wish of paramount importance will come true
- Feelings of tremendous joy
- An emotional journey is almost over or will come to fruition
- Contentment

TEN OF CUPS

- Happiness and contentment
- A sense of permanence and future purpose
- It often suggests starting a family
- The sense of harmony
- Also suggests marriage
- Can also indicate responsibilities within a community

SWORDS SUIT– deals with how a person speaks, how one perceives the world, an individual's belief system, how one makes decisions, and understand things. The suit of Swords has the most problematic points in the tarot deck, but it is the nature of air and the mind.

Court Cards:

PAGE OF SWORDS

- Has a quality of wit and carelessness

- Also suggests immature thoughts

KNIGHT OF SWORDS

- Communicator
- Someone who loves to learn and interested in new ideas
- Very expressive or talkative

QUEEN OF SWORDS

- Advocate
- Someone who has high principles
- Doesn't compromise or negotiate
- Someone who is emotional and critical

KING OF SWORDS

- Enforcer
- Someone who upholds the laws or values
- One who leads and decides
- Sometimes unsympathetic

Pip Cards

ACE OF SWORDS (1)

- Inevitable and irrevocable change
- Awakening of mental powers
- Conflict can somehow arise at the start but are ultimately beneficial to the growth of the person

- Also called the sword of polarity or the sword of absolute knowledge
- It's a card of mind empowerment

TWO OF SWORDS

- Stalemate; ambiguity
- Nothing can move or change
- Suggests great tension or deep hostility
- A person must make choices
- Having an inner focus in oneself
- Can also be about denial

THREE OF SWORDS

- Quarrels and conflict
- A period of challenges or flux for relationships
- It also suggests that something sad or painful must be allowed to work something out
- Heartbreak or pain
- Disappointment; delusions
- Also, suggest healing and assessment of the situation

FOUR OF SWORDS

- A need for rest or retreat after stress
- A time for reconciliation after tension
- Recuperation

- Suggests peace despite turmoil
- Postponement of decisions

FIVE OF SWORDS

- Also known as the boundary card
- Indicates contradiction
- Pride must be swallowed
- Limitations must be recognized before further progress can be made
- Suggests that a person must work within the framework of that situation

SIX OF SWORDS

- A card of harmony
- A period of calm after great anxiety
- Release of tension
- A peaceful journey towards smoother waters
- Also, suggest that a person should physically move away from an unpleasant environment
- Indicates physical travel or postponement of decision because the mind is inactive

SEVEN OF SWORDS

- A need for evasion and avoidance of direct confrontation in order to achieve a goal
- One must use his/her logical thinking, tact, and diplomacy instead of aggression

- Avoidance of conflict
- Sometimes known as the card of deceit or secrets
- Sometimes not wanting to face something or someone who hides the truth

EIGHT OF SWORDS

- Fear of moving out of a situation in relationships
- Can also suggest a situation of tension but in this case, the choices are perfectly conscious
- It also talks about how one's perceptions block the will
- There could be a fear of change
- The belief system could get a person stuck which is why the card suggests that an individual must think of something or perceive something in a different way

NINE OF SWORDS

- A time in which the mind is experiencing fears due to bad though
- Nightmares and fantasies trouble the mind of the individual
- Can also mean that the end of the mental struggle is near
- Anxiety and being overwhelmed
- There's a sense of worry and doom

TEN OF SWORDS

- The end of a painful situation or state
- There emerges an ability to see a situation practicality
- A fresh start is expected
- The start of the new cycle is about to begin which brings new hope
- A new horizon is near despite the previous struggles

PENTACLES SUIT – the suit of Pentacles is not just about money or financial matters; it's also about tangible or material things. It's also about the practical and pragmatic side, the stability and security in the physical world. It's also about how one's belief system, spirituality, and creative tendencies play out in one's life.

Court Cards:

PAGE OF PENTACLES

- Apprentice
- Someone who has a plan and undertakes a long term activity
- Indicates new beginnings and a new perspective
- Someone who is earnest and grounded

KNIGHT OF PENTACLES

- Worker
- Someone who is reliable and more mechanical
- Resourceful

- Doesn't move fast and takes his time in doing something
- Someone who exert steady effort to achieve something

QUEEN OF PENTACLES

- Nurturer
- Represents constancy and comfort
- Someone who is self – employed and one who takes charge of their own life
- Calm but not complacent
- Industrious

KING OF PENTACLES

- Entrepreneur
- Somebody who knows how to make money and provides security
- Someone who knows how to build things that will last

Pip Cards:

ACE OF PENTACLES (1)

- Acquisition of material wealth is possible
- A startup financial aid is may be available
- New opportunities that are related to work or home

- New growth in every aspect of one's life (home, health, career)

TWO OF PENTACLES

- There is instability in financial matters
- There'll be optimism and enthusiasm which balances out the anxieties when it comes to financial matters
- Transition
- There could be some sort of instability but not chaotic
- Flexible and can have many options, the key is to be open

THREE OF PENTACLES

- A satisfactory period for a person
- Work completion at the start
- Construction of a basic structure
- Can indicate effective partnerships or collaboration
- Has a firm foundation

FOUR OF PENTACLES

- Danger in overdependence
- Nothing is lost, nothing gained
- Resistance to change
- Focuses on self – preservation or maintaining one's position

FIVE OF PENTACLES

- Financial loss and difficulty
- Loss of luck especially in health
- Loss of self - confidence
- Expectation of failure
- Deprivation mentality
- Can indicate a lack of spiritual connection

SIX OF PENTACLES

- Generous assistance from friend or employer
- Suggest a situation in which there is abundance worth sharing
- Shared resources
- Mutually beneficial

SEVEN OF PENTACLES

- Tough choices need to be made between material wealth and unpredictable opportunities
- Focuses about patience and taking time to make things happen
- There's the availability of options
- Suggests reevaluation and can also indicate a lack of motivation

EIGHT OF PENTACLES

- Beginner coaching or commencing a new endeavor in another field

- Rearrangement or realignment of priorities in any aspect
- One should take a new focus

NINE OF PENTACLES

- A card of unrivaled comfort and satisfaction
- There'll be a reward for industry or material gains
- Confidence in one's abilities
- Someone who celebrates life
- Appreciation for the good thing that is happening in one's life
- Someone who is self - reliant

TEN OF PENTACLES

- Financial security and base for a family
- A new phase in life is about to come
- Denotes values of society, cultural traditions, morals and marriage (something that is unlikely to change or something that is secure)

Court Cards

There are 16 personality cards or commonly known in tarot as the court cards. Court cards have these following characteristics that you need to keep in mind:

- **Court Cards stay true to their element**

They live, breathe, and die in the nature of the suit that they represent. Say for example if a court card shows up, and it belongs to the suit of pentacles, you can expect that this card cares about practicality, it's grounded and deals with the concrete side of any issue since pentacles are of earth elements. The court card belonging to the wands suit represents challenges, creativity, and the self – expressive quality.

- **Court Cards are not gender or age specific**

Court cards express energies, but it doesn't pertain to a certain age or gender. Say, for example, you pulled the Queen of Cups it doesn't necessarily mean that it's about a woman; it could mean that it's about somebody who has characteristics, reactions or experiences related to what the Queen of Cups card is denoting. It can be quite tricky sometimes to not look at the gender or age that is being depicted in the card.

- **Court Cards reflects the level of experience with a certain element**

The Pages card within each suit are the least mature, the Knights are more adventurous, the Queens serve as the channel or vehicles in which the element can be fully expressed, and the Kings are the leaders or masters because it has characteristics that like to have control over the element and sometimes are personally creative with the element. You have to keep in mind though, that there's no such thing as a good card or a bad card, there's no absolute positive or negative card, there could be a positive or negative approach depending on the situation, but there's no card on the deck that is intrinsically good or bad.

- **Court Cards work best if the question is properly phrased**

How you phrase the subject's query or question will give you as a reader a format or context in which the question will be answered. Court cards can mean different things, so instead of just randomly pulling out a card, it's best to have a proper context or determine a certain aspect.

Chapter Nine
Reading a Tarot Card for the Day

The notion of pulling a card every day works best if you really take the time to 'feel' your cards or sit with your tarot deck for at least a couple of minutes every morning so you can sort of feel the energy within these cards. The idea behind this is to focus or become aware of the kind of energy you have for that particular day. It's not necessarily about programming your day or having a planned activity, but it's more of having that sense of both the positive and negative aspects because it can also affect how the cards will show up. This chapter will also cover how to interpret meaning that's "not" in a reading or patterns that aren't obvious.

How to Read a Tarot Card for the Day

For you to be able to interpret a card you pulled for a particular day, you have to pay attention to the different sides of the card and observe the energy you feel for yourself or with other people. Say for example you pulled out a King of Cups card; you can the first layout its literal meaning like this card is someone who is a nurturer, who cares deeply and can be strongly attached to things or people they have a relationship with. Another kind of meaning you could be getting from this card could also pertain to someone who is protective or quite controlling; there could also be an abundance of emotion in general.

You can relate the meanings or characteristics of the card in your experiences throughout the day. Of course, not everyone has the luxury to recap their whole day or record every significant thing that happens (if any), but you have to be aware of things like the energy or characteristics of the card and how it played out its different attributes during the day. You can learn from that so you can have a better understanding of how you can use it in the future whenever you're doing a card reading for the day.

So, basically there's no formula or standard method even for expert tarot readers when it comes to interpreting a card for the day, some books or guides may tell you tips or guiding principles but it's clearly up to you on how you interpret things and relate the energies or events that happened to you with the card you pulled for that particular day, sometimes you just have to be consciously aware of it or maybe do some mental notes. The context doesn't really matter, and according to most tarot readers, the symbols of tarot cards are all parts of our lives' constellations – the more you can define and depict events in your day to day life, the more you'll be able to understand and recognize the energy from a tarot card.

What's Not in the Tarot Reading

When you're doing a reading, one of the first things you should do is to scan the cards and see if the majority of cards are in the major arcana or minor arcana. Below are some examples of a situation that is not in a tarot reading and what it could mean to the interpretation or impact of the message:

Example #1: Major and Minor Arcana (Questions about Spiritual Aspect)

If the cards predominantly belong to the major arcana in a spread, the message is most likely related to a spiritual path of an individual or some kind of growth in an individual's soul. It can also mean an internal processor change in a psychological or spiritual level.

- What's Not in the Reading: The Minor Arcana

Minor Arcana are composed of tarot cards that are relating to everyday life or relating to situations with people as well as how an individual is processing the daily life and the struggles that come along with it. Since the sample spread doesn't have any minor arcana, it simply means that the message is not about your subject's processing in their daily life's circumstances. You can assume that the focus is about the inner growth or mental and spiritual development or connection (if the question is about relationships). Simply put, if there are no minor arcana in your spread, the message is centered on a much deeper or profound level that can affect one's soul or mental growth as well as conscience.

Example #2: Cups Card and Pentacles Card (Questions about Relationships)

One of the most common examples is when your subject asks you questions about relationships. Often times they would like to know the current status of their romantic relationship, and usually, the key indicator in the realm of relationship is a

Water (cups) card because it deals with the emotional element or feelings that one has for another individual. Now, what if a client asks about relationship stuff and they have pulled no cups or water cards? As an example, we'll use the pentacles card.

- What's Not in the Reading: The Cups Card

When there's no cups card in a reading, it doesn't necessarily mean that there's no emotional bond or connection but perhaps the connection for a certain individual is channeled in something that is important, or it's in a different focus of the relationship that's not about sharing emotion. Say for example, your subject pulled pentacles card in a reading, it could mean that the relationship at the given time is centered on grounding areas that are not emotional – it focuses perhaps on a more tangible aspect that the relationship has created like the possessions you bought together or it can also mean that they have a more practical or reliable relationship. Since the pentacles card has an earth (ground bound) element to it, the relationship can also mean that it's sort of a work in progress for both individuals involved.

Example #3: Water Cards (Questions about Career)

If your client asks you about career-related topics, the suits or cards relating to work are usually pentacles (how to manifest it in the physical realm) as well as wands (because it relates to one's drive or passion that one needs to accomplish a goal). So typically the cards you're looking for is a Pentacles or Wands card but what if your client didn't pull any of that and instead pulled out cards like our examples.

So say, for example, your subject pulled out nothing but water cards, you can immediately assume that there's something going on about this individual in an emotional level or they're working through something with a purpose. You can also consider their feelings like if your subject probably feels working in a project that may have an impact on their spiritual or emotional aspect or that particular project may relate to helping others and/or involves creativity.

You also have to think about if there's an emotional basis or drive to feel fulfillment on a particular goal or if your subject may need to adjust their path to fulfill something or monetize something. It may also involve a creative aspect, so you need to think about if your subject is infusing creativity in their work or perhaps they wanted to express more creativity in what they do but may not be able to have that freedom in their current jobs – so you can suggest that they could change jobs to find a more fulfilling career or something like that.

- What's Not in the Reading: The Pentacles and Wands Card

If you or your subject didn't pull any pentacles and/or wands card, as a reader, you have to automatically say to your subject that he/she is focusing on other things or have been dealing with other things not related to work. Perhaps there's some kind of way that they're channeling their career goal through themselves or utilizing themselves that may not be related to a tangible work.

Example #4: Sword Cards (Questions about Career)

Here's another example regarding questions about career. If no pentacle or wand cards showed up and there are only Sword (air) cards on the spread it can mean the following:

- The individual could have a potentially good idea or has a spark of inspiration
- There's some level of truth or information, and the person wants to manifest it but hasn't' done yet
- There's a chance that they might have lots of ideas, but it only stays in their mental sphere and may not have been manifested into tangible results yet
- Since there are no wands in the spread, they may not know how to move a particular thought or idea forward

So if you see a lot of swords in terms of career and there are no pentacles or wands, basically it only tells you that your subject may have an idea that he/she wants to do but can't for some reason. You can advise him/her to maybe just give it a try so the idea can hopefully become real or manifest in the physical world.

Example #5: Masculine and Feminine Cards

There are two polarities – masculine and feminine. Feminine cards (Water/Cups and Earth/Pentacles) have characteristics of being more receptive, introverted, security, stability, don't want to take any risks, and it deals with a more internal world. Masculine cards (Fire/Wands and Air/Swords) on the other hand, are more extroverted cards, active, and more action – oriented.

- What's Not in the Reading: Feminine Cards

If for example, the question is about relationships and you only see masculine cards, you can assume that the emotional or security aspect is not the focus of the message. It can rather have an outgoing aspect to it if you pulled either a sword card or wand card; the relationship could be more direct and perhaps aims to move forward or quickly.

Chapter Ten
Tarot as a Spiritual Doorway

<u>Using the Cards for Creativity, Ritual, and Prayer</u>

Most people are drawn to the Tarot for one reason—to divine the future. And as a divinatory tool, the cards have no true equal. It seems a shame, however, to relegate your decks to Oracle Only status when the beauty and poetry of their landscapes make for such a creative and soul-enticing ride.

I have decks all over the house; I am frequently seen carrying, shuffling, studying, fiddling. The artwork of my various acquisitions serves as a constant source of inspiration and invention; I'm pretty sure this book alone has been good for several dozen gaze-and-ponder sessions. In this chapter, I'm going to offer you ways to work with the cards outside of a psychic reading—and discover all the places you can go with a deck in your hand, even when you don't have any particular destination in mind.

A Cosmic String around Your Finger

A life lived consciously is a magical one. Conscious living is a matter of paying attention —to our thoughts, words, actions, and to the signs and signals from the Universe around us. Miracles and serendipitous events become the norm when you walk in the world with that kind of awareness. One of my favorite ways to cultivate miracle consciousness is using the

Tarot as a daily reminder—choosing one card in the morning as a focal point for the whole day.

Shuffle your deck and pull a single card, asking for guidance, focus, or for whatever your guides want you to know. Put the card somewhere you can see it as you go about your routine—on your altar, the kitchen counter, the table in the entryway where you drop your keys and sort your mail. Then watch not only for the message of the card to unfold throughout the course of your day but also for specific images from that card to show up, quite tangibly.

Draw a Card and Cast a Spell

A Tarot is an indispensable tool for ritual and spell work, as it can heighten one's ability to visualize and emotionally connect to unformed goals and desires. Picturing something into being is a method of manifestation that has been used since the earliest days of our cave-dwelling ancestors; known as sympathetic magic, employing images of the desired object or experience in order to draw it to you is an ancient and powerful form of ritual intent.

Spells and rituals using the Tarot can be as simple or as extravagant as you wish. I have danced the night away in a room aflame with candles and moonlight, around an altar draped with velvet and heaped with flowers, crystals, and twenty-one different Tarot images of the High Priestess. It took me days to come down to Earth from that one!

And I have lit a single, tiny, hand-dipped beeswax taper, studied the image of the Six of Pentacles by its flickering light, and asked Spirit to help me with a medical bill I had no way of paying. Two days later a check arrived in the mail from my insurance company for a claim I had sent in six months prior (and had all but written off because of the time lag) that was, to the dollar, the exact amount I needed to pay the bill.

Because of the transcendent nature of the imagery, the Tarot is a natural for inciting the subconscious to action and stimulating the miracle consciousness required for manifestation. In simpler terms? You have to believe it before you'll see it—and the Tarot can help you create inwardly, on the mental plane, so that what you dream of can manifest outwardly in the physical.

The trick is to choose cards that not only visually depict what you desire but also evoke the strongest emotional response to the wished-for outcome. For instance, the Ace of Pentacles for some might illustrate great wealth and security; for others, a single disk doesn't add up, so the Nine or Ten of Pentacles is their card of choice for a money ritual.

Following are a few of my personal favorite Tarot cards for visualization and ritual intent. I use these cards because I'm so strongly drawn to and affected by their imagery. If you don't have the decks that these specific cards are from, no big deal— I'm only listing them here to use as a reference, if you'd like. Remember, trust your own emotions and instincts first and choose cards from whichever deck or decks spark you the most.

Money: The Six and Nine of Pentacles from the Robin Wood Tarot; the Empress and the Queen of Pentacles from the Hanson-Roberts Tarot; the Sun and Fortune from the Voyager Tarot

Business: The Emperor and the Eight of Pentacles from Robin Wood; the Three and the King of Pentacles from Hanson-Roberts; the Ace of Worlds and the Eight of Crystals from Voyager

Love: The Two of Cups and the Four of Wands from Robin Wood; the Ace of Cups and the Lovers from Hanson-Roberts; the Six of Worlds and the Three of Cups from Voyager

Happiness: The Three of Cups and the Empress from Robin Wood; the Nine and Ten of Cups from Hanson-Roberts; the Ace and Nine of Cups from Voyager

Health: Temperance and the Star from Robin Wood; Strength and the Empress from Hanson-Roberts; the Woman of Worlds and Balance from Voyager.

Personal Power: The High Priestess and Judgment from Robin Wood; the Magician and Justice from Hanson-Roberts; the Woman of Wands and the Woman of Crystals from Voyager

Creativity: The Three of Pentacles and the Page of Cups from Robin Wood; the Sun and the Seven

Of Cups from Hanson-Roberts; the Child of Cups and Art from Voyager

Spiritual Connection: The Fool and the Hermit from Robin Wood; the Ace of Swords and the Ace of Rods from Hanson-Roberts; the Ten of Wands and the Universe from Voyager

A single card can direct your subconscious to powerful outcomes; placed in deliberate combinations, the cards, and their imagery can map the story of your greatest desires. Following are three mini rituals you can do, using the Tarot as your point of focus and realization. You can perform these rituals as they are written, or expand on them as you like, such as burning corresponding incense, adding appropriate crystals, flowers, or other symbolic objects, working with the energies of different days or Moon cycles, and of course, casting a magic circle. However you choose to do them, do them with reverence and intent, as you would any sacred act.

An Abundance Spell

Use this spell for increasing your financial income, for meeting a particular financial obligation, or for creating a windfall.

Supplies
1 green candle
Powdered cinnamon
1 Tarot card that represents wealth and financial abundance to you—the Six, Nine, or Ten of Pentacles; the Queen of Pentacles or the Empress if you're a woman; the King of Pentacles or the Emperor if you're a man; or any other card in your deck that invokes the energy of wealth for you
Coins and paper currency, either real or play

Lay the Tarot card face up; surround it with the coins and paper money. Place the green candle at the head of the Tarot card, and light it. Focus on the image of the card, imagining your income increasing easily and joyfully, your bank balances growing effortlessly, your bills paid in full, etc. Spend as much time on this visualization as you can, without your attention wavering. Then sprinkle small pinches of the cinnamon on the candle flame and repeat these words:

Coins of silver, and of gold,
Bring me fortune, wealth untold.
Riches come through every door
To make my money ten times more.

Continue visualizing as long as you can, sprinkling more cinnamon if you desire (the sparks are like magical little fireflies!), then proclaim the spell completely, and thank God, Goddess, or the Universe for answered prayer. Either let the candle burn out or snuff the flame and keep what remains of the candle (wrapped in one of the paper bills and tied with a green or gold cord) on your altar or somewhere sacred until your wish manifests.

A Spell for Love

Use this spell for attracting love to you or for strengthening an existing partnership. This should go without saying, but I'm saying it anyway: Do not do this with energy or intent of manipulating anyone's affections. This is a ritual for divine love, not coercion.

Supplies

2 red or pink candles

1 white candle

Rose petals, fresh or dried

Heart shaped confetti

1 significator card, representing you 1 significator card representing your current partner or the kind of partner you would like to attract

1 Tarot card representing true love—for example, the Ace or Two of Cups, the Four of Wands, the Lovers, etc.

Lay the significator cards side by side, leaving enough space between for a third card; set the love card aside for now. You may place your significator on the left or the right as you wish—if energetic placement feels right, then put the feminine to the left and the masculine to the right; if you want the two characters looking at each other, organize them accordingly; or simply trust your first instincts as to who goes where. (Someone once suggested placing the significator cards according to which side of the bed each person sleeps on. I say, whatever works!) Sprinkle the rose petals and confetti in a circle around the cards, or, if you really want to make an impression, create a heart shape. Place the red/pink candles at the head of the significator cards; place the white candle at the head of the empty space.

Light the red/pink candles. Focus on the cards and visualize yourself and your partner as two strong, independent, healthy, loving individuals, spiritually grounded, happy in your own lives, respectful of yourselves and one another, each desiring a healthy and committed partnership. Take your time with this; make it a physical and emotional realization. Then when you feel ready, place the love card in between, and light the white candle, speaking these words aloud:

Lord and Lady, King and Queen,
Magician, Priestess, love between.
This bond be sacred, two in one,
Heart and soul 'til the time are done.

Now, visualize the kind of relationship you desire, the wonderful experiences you'll share together, the level of intimacy, and connection between you, the spiritual and creative horizons you'll explore. As before, make this as real and emotionally powerful as possible and concentrate for as long as you comfortably can. Then proclaim the spell complete and give thanks for answered prayer; let the candles burn out of their own accord, or snuff the flames and keep what's left of the candles together, wrapped in a red or pink cloth with some of the rose petals, on your altar or somewhere sacred until your wish manifests.

A Transformation Ritual

This little spell is wonderful for any circumstance with which you may be struggling—health issues, financial problems, relationship woes, etc. Healing and release may be just a candle flame away. . . .

Supplies
1 black candle
1 white candle

1 Tarot card representing your challenge, and 1 card representing what you would like the situation to become. Here are a few examples:

Nine of Swords/the Sun (for transforming depression, worry)

Four or Five of Pentacles/Nine of Pentacles (for financial problems)

Five of Pentacles or Ten of Swords/Strength or King of Pentacles (for health issues)

Five of Wands or Cups/Two of Cups or Four of Wands (for relationship troubles)

Eight of Swords, Five of Wands or the Tower/the Star or Temperance (for anxiety, crisis, chronic drama)

Place the black candle on the left with the challenge card below it, face up; the white candle on the right with the card of transformation face down. Light the black candle and focus on the image of the challenge card, thinking about your situation and its energy. Imagine channeling that energy into the candle, infusing the very wax with the problem you're facing. Then, when you're ready, speak these words aloud:

Candle black, candle white
Heal this darkness with your light.
I now release this plight to be
Transformed by love, so I am free.

Now, turn the challenge card face down, deliberately; light the white candle and turn the transformation card face up. Focus on the image of this card, and this time, infuse yourself with the energy—of health, harmony, happiness, prosperity, whatever it is you are wishing for. Imagine the candle flames burning your challenge to cinders and charging you and your desire with vital life force. Make this visualization count; let yourself experience the healing and transformation in your mind, body, and emotions. Stay with it as long as you can; when it feels complete, proclaim the spell as such, and give thanks for answered prayer. Then either let the candles burn out (if you safely can, this is best), or snuff the flames and take what remains of the candles, bind them together with black thread, and bury them in the ground, preferably of your property.

Om and Amen

A spell is really nothing more than a ritualized prayer, with specific actions and accoutrements that correspond to the spoken request. For those times when there's no time to do ritual or spell work, the Tarot can up the ante on your prayer power tenfold. How? Prayer is a concentration; concentration is attention focused on a single object or idea. The Tarot's symbolism sparks not only the intellect but also the emotions, creating the perfect combination of inspiration and intent, all wrapped up in a neat little package.

A client of mine, new to her spiritual path, had no idea how to pray or to whom; a self-described recovering Catholic, she had long ago given up on the conventional idea of God. She did, however, like the idea of angels, and I suggested she try using the card of Temperance as a focus for her efforts. That was five years ago, and she still talks to that card every morning and carries the loving and familiar image in her mind throughout the day.

I have a gorgeous fifty-year-old pine cabinet from Mexico, filled with crystals, seashells, feathers, stars, tiny lamps that burn jewel-colored oils, and many representations of the God and Goddess, some found, some purchased, some gifted to me by people I love. This is the site of years of daily prayer sessions and many an impromptu mini-ritual; when I open the scrollwork doors and light the lamps, I am immediately lifted, held, and graced by the collective energy of every wish and every gratitude ever spoken there. This is my church, and often I will go and simply stand there, soaking in the delicious vibration, much as I imagine people sit in quiet chapels or synagogues, just hanging out at the feet of God.

Inside on the left, near a delicate silver goblet and a Ukrainian Easter egg, is the card of the High Priestess from my first copy of the Robin Wood Tarot. (I am currently on my sixth copy— this deck gets a lot of use in my house!) And to the right, beside a deer antler and an Aztec Sun, is the Magician, her soul mate; these two visually conjure the God and the Goddess for me, as clearly as if they'd stepped straight from the heavens to stand at my side. And when I'm in need of connection, inspiration, comfort, or support, I choose an appropriate card from the deck that resides among the crystals and seashells, and I meditate on its imagery in the lamplight, watched over by my magical guardians.

I also use the Tarot as a meditation tool with my Neuro-Linguistic Programming (NLP) clients. When someone is blocked, unable to manifest or create positive change in their lives, nine times out of ten it's because they have no frame of reference for what they want, and therefore, no ability to visualize their desired outcome. Using the Voyager deck, i'll have my client go through the cards face up, choosing the images that incite the feeling they're going for. Sometimes we'll play with putting their chosen cards in a particular order or pattern; other times, we'll pare the pile down to one or two of the most dramatic representations and spend awhile focusing, discussing, imagining. Then I have my client study the cards in silence for a time, meditating on the imagery, drawing the emotional energy into their bodies with every breath, claiming that energy as their own.

By the time they leave the session, my client has both a visual and an emotional link to their desired future, something I call a barometer — any choice that faces them, any idea that wants pursuing, can be held up to the image to see if it fits energetically. (Would the King of Wands choose this particular career path? If the Hierophant attended tomorrow's board meeting, how would he handle the sales presentation? Does my current relationship fit the landscape of the Three of Cups?) If so, through conscious action toward the choice or idea, coupled with prayer and continued spiritual focus, seen and unseen wheels alike are set in motion that turn dreams into absolute reality.

Chapter Eleven

Bringing All Your Mystic Skills Together to Get the Results That You Want

<u>Interesting Facts, FAQ, and Tips for Tarot Cards</u>

There are a number of interesting facts out there that many people are not aware of. While you are learning all there is to know about Tarot Cards; you might as well take some time to learn these great facts.

In the art of divination, the use of Tarot cards is the most practiced throughout the world. There are some out there that refer to the Tarot cards as The Book of Divination of the Gypsies.

The Tarot cards have been around since the Renaissance and are believed to have started in Northern Italy.

The Tarot cards were brought to Europe by the Gypsies.

Arcana means secret or mystery.

There are thousands of decks of Tarot cards for different interests that are out there.

Tarot cards were first used for telling the future in 1785.

The original use of Tarot cards was as a card game.

There are a number of questions that you might have when it comes to Tarot cards. Here are some of the most common questions.

What is the length of an average reading? The average reading should take about 15 minutes. This is dependent on the depth of the reading.

Does someone have to give me a Tarot card deck for it to work? The simple answer to this question is NO. You will find that some of the best decks you will find are the ones you select for yourself.

Is reading Tarot cards dangerous? The basic answer to this is NO. There is no calling of evil spirits involved in Tarot cards.

Do you have to be psychic to be able to read Tarot cards? The answer to this question is YES. Now keep in mind that everyone out there has a certain level of psychic abilities if they Know how to tap into them.

While there are a number of questions that you can ask the Tarot cards, there are some questions that you should never ever ask the Tarot cards. Here is a list of questions that you should not ask the Tarot cards, as well as the reasons why.

Any question about an ex. You want to make sure that you have positive energies when you are reading cards. Asking questions about someone that you might not have positive emotions about can skew the reading.

Do not ask a question that does not apply to you specifically. You have to ask the Tarot cards about you specifically. You will not be able to get a clear reading for someone that is not in the room.

Specific questions. You can ask generalized questions, but the cards are not going to be able to give your specific names, dates, or times.

Yes or No questions. The Tarot cards are a guide: you want to find more generalized questions that they can map out for you.

When you will die, once again, this is a more specific question than you should not be asking. This is also a question that the Tarot cards just cannot answer. What might be accurate today could change tomorrow depending on if you have made a choice that will change your current path.

Am I pregnant? There are far easier ways to find the answer to this question. Besides, this is a yes or no question and so cannot be asked to the cards.

Now that you have all this information, you might want to look for a few tips and tricks to help you get started on your Tarot card journey. We have put together a few that might help you out as you are starting out.

Learn to phrase the question. You cannot get specific information from the cards, so you will want to know how to ask the questions. For example, you would not ask how many kids you will have. Instead, you would want to phrase the question as what is the potential for having kids.

Do not second-guess yourself. There are too many times that beginners doubt their reading and will do a reading over and over again. This doubt will cloud the cards and skew the results.

Start simple. There are those out there that want to jump with both feet first. This is not the best idea when it comes to Tarot card reading. You want to progress naturally, which means that you need to keep it simple at first until you are more comfortable with what you are doing.

Learn one a day. Draw one card a day and learn everything you can about that card. You might want to keep a journal and put each card in the journal. Generally, you will want to put in how it made you feel, what it means, and later on, you can put what the reverse of the card means. As you progress, you will fill your journal and learn the cards.

The main idea behind Tarot cards is to be able to give a great reading while having a great time. Just keep in mind that the position of the cards as well as if they are right-side up or upside down makes a difference. There are different meanings for each card and in each category. We just wanted you to start with the basics, and then you should be able to expand upon these basics. Only you will know when you are ready to expand.

Every person is different, so the rate of acceleration is different for each person. If you are finding that you are not able to get the concepts right away, it is fine. Some of the greatest tarot card readers out there took years just to understand the basics.

You will simply want to make sure that you understand one concept prior to moving on to something else.

Chapter Twelve
Setting boundaries

While setting boundaries isn't the sexiest topic in the world, it is, in my experience, the most necessary exercise in any magical practice. This is true for many reasons. People are coming for readings in deep vulnerability; they are asking questions and revealing parts of themselves that they oftentimes conceal even from their closest friends. There is a responsibility you hold as a reader to the people coming to you, and the sooner you define your boundaries, the cleaner your practice will be.

When I first started reading tarot, boundaries were a foreign concept to me. I took late night phone calls, confused professional relationships with personal friendships, had no recourse for last minute cancellations, spent unpaid hours responding to e-mails from clients who had follow-up questions, spent a lot of time worrying about what people thought of their readings and feeling guilty if I gave them unwelcome information. Everything i've learned about boundaries over the course of my experience reading tarot is a product of crossing them.

It took time for me to understand boundaries as an act of self-love and self-preservation and something that makes you and the people around you feel safe. No one enjoys feeling like they are getting something out of obligation, and honoring your boundaries builds a trust that allows people to believe when you say yes, you're all in. I believed that if I said no to something that didn't feel right—the last minute booking that would stretch me too thin, an event opportunity at a loud club full of drunk people on Halloween—I would lose something. It was fear-based decision making that did me no favors besides expertise in what not to do. Read on.

Dependence and Attachment

While there is nothing more rewarding than working with repeat clients, it is important to stay conscious of the nature of the attachment being formed. Just because someone asks for reading doesn't mean you need to give it to them, or that it is appropriate at that time. I've had people contact me a week after their last reading asking for another. It is clear, in situations like that, that they either didn't get the answer they wanted or are relying too heavily on the cards to make decisions. Sometimes, people request readings to look into short-term issues that will resolve themselves within days (fight with a partner, a job interview, etc.). I do not offer readings as Band-Aids for panic. To me, it feels exploitative and unethical. I will not capitalize on someone's fear or desperation. There are readers who I love and respect who will do quick reads for people in a pinch, but it does not feel right to me personally. That is my boundary.

Not everyone is happy with me at the moment, but it has built long-term trust with my clients. They know I will not always take their money just because they are willing to give it to me.

Honoring Your Time

Don't get overwhelmed with the idea of charging for readings. You may not be looking to read professionally and therefore, exchanging money for readings is not relevant to you. However, to give a reading is an expenditure of energy, and to give energy without receiving anything in return, forges an imbalance for both the reader and the querist. When starting out, someone offering their time to help you practice may be exchanged enough. However, when you become more comfortable in your ability to give readings, set up some kind of trade with the people coming to you. Money is just energy, and by no means, the only form of currency. The barter system is a beautiful thing. You can trade reading for dinner, a piece of art, a bottle of wine, a massage, and the list goes on.

If you intend to read professionally, it is essential to place a monetary value on your time. Oftentimes clients will e-mail after the reading with one more question or want to follow up on things that came up during the reading. Schedule a follow-up appointment for a pro-rated amount (I offer 15-minute follow-ups) rather than sending a long e-mail or getting on a late night phone call.

It took months of people cancelling appointments at the last minute or not showing up altogether, arguing with me about price and giving follow-up readings for free for me to decide to implement things like a set rate and a cancellation policy. This was scary. Any time we defend our worth—monetary or otherwise—we are probably going to scare the shit out of ourselves a little bit. I already felt like I won the lottery by being able to read tarot professionally and didn't want to push it, but nothing was lost. No one fought me or questioned it. I didn't lose clients or get wiped off the face of the earth. Same story when I raised my rates, cut down on events, and stopped offering in-home readings. Even my fussiest Manhattan clients made the voyage to Brooklyn.

Knowing Your Limitations

The scope of what the tarot can provide a person will never cease to floor me in its expansiveness. The healing and transformation i've seen occur from readings has brought me to tears over and over again. But—and this is a big but—there are indispensable forms of treatment that are not interchangeable with a reading. Chances are you are not a mental health professional. And even if you are, if someone is coming to you for reading and not counsel on their mental health, then stay in your own lane.

Part of honoring the responsibility others entrust in you is to know when to call it. I've had clients come to me supremely fucked up by readers who gave unsolicited and uninformed advice: recovering addicts told that total sobriety wasn't necessary, people with mental illness advised to get off their medication, cancer patients instructed to change their treatment. I have personal thoughts on all of these matters, but a client isn't coming to you for advice, they are coming for channeled, intuitive guidance.

Sometimes, people just need help beyond a reading's capacity. Anything can come up in a reading—mental illness, childhood trauma, sexual abuse, grief, physical ailments—but that does not mean that you personally have the tools to deal with any and all of these matters. I certainly do not. I do, however, have an arsenal of healers whom I trust and refer people to. This includes therapists, body workers, Reiki practitioners, hypnotists, acupuncturists, mediums, breathworkers, yoga instructors, shamans, intuitive, other tarot readers and, yes, doctors and psychiatrists. If someone's needs exceed your ability to meet them, it is useful to have resources on hand for them and important to guide them to the help they need when you cannot give it. An extreme scenario of this is if someone comes in presenting a danger to themselves or others, they should be immediately referred to a physician. Usually, a client will just need ongoing support in continuing their work. Many readers go on to train in additional modalities to provide a more holistic healing experience for their clients and see them through their process.

Self-Care

There is an agreement you make stepping into healership to soften the veil of your ego to feel someone else's experience truly. But once the reading is over, this energy must be released. You are a messenger for the information of the cards; what they deliver to the client is not your fault or your burden. Oftentimes, reading is just the beginning for a person, as it lays out a map of what they need to do in order to reach their highest potential. This is where the aforementioned resources are a valuable way of further supporting your client in the now what?Space they sometimes find themselves in.

You diminish your use if you hold on to reading after it is over. Healers have various ways of shaking off excess energy after giving a reading—from prayer and meditation to dancing to taking a bath to go for a walk to watching trashy TV. It doesn't have to be super spiritual; it just has to work for you.

Consent

This one's a biggie, but it is also very simple. If someone doesn't ask for a reading, don't give them one. If you offer someone reading and they don't explicitly say yes, don't give them one. I've had people come for readings pissed off, skeptical, reluctant, insisting that this was all bullshit. But they still came. They travelled to my space to receive a reading. And, despite their hesitation, when I asked if they wanted to move forward with the reading, they said yes. It's easy to get a little over-enthusiastic at the beginning when we are learning the cards and want to offer them to everyone, and that's largely positive. But respecting other people's boundaries is paramount to a practice that is rooted in integrity. Only yes means yes, y'all.

Chapter Thirteen
Tarot Reading FAQ

When giving a reading, what do I do first?

Take some time with the person before jumping in to pull cards for them. Depending on where you are, have your setup ready—the bare minimum of which is two seats with a surface in between to lay the cards out. Think about the best way to make you and the client feel comfortable, whether it is engaging in some chit chat or starting off with a quiet moment. I tend to ask my clients a few innocuous questions at the beginning—where they're coming from, inquiring about something they're wearing, how about this fucking weather, huh?—before jumping into the realness. For returning clients, it's nice to touch base briefly, and for new clients, it aids in snapping them out of any anxiety or awkwardness they may feel coming into a reading.

Do you talk to a client at length before a reading starts? If so, about what?

This is something that you, as the reader, can decide upon beforehand or leave up to your client. I have some people come in, and they won't say a word before we start either because they're skeptical and want to test me or are otherwise unwilling to give details about what's going on. After the aforementioned small talk is over (run time of which is approximately two minutes), I ask if there is anything they want their reading to be focused on or based around, any area or aspect of their life where they feel like they need more clarity or direction. When people come uncertain of what to focus on, I advise them to ask about the matter that is sitting heaviest in their heart. I also let them know reading can be left completely open, and we can begin with a general overview. It is worth noting that a general reading becomes specific very quickly, but that we let the cards decide what to focus on rather than setting the intention beforehand. This is the case one in every five times, with people typically coming for readings aware of what their intention is going into it, and willing to share that with you. I used to be scared of the people who didn't say anything before a reading started, but I have come to prefer that over clients who spend the first twenty minutes of their reading explaining their circumstances in-depth. This is not a therapy session, and getting bogged down in the details of a story is not necessary for you as the reader or helpful for them as the client. If they do want to share information, I try to limit it to five minutes of conversation before drawing cards. I have found this is a healthy balance of starting reading at an appropriate level of depth—you don't have to do the time-wasting guess-work of it seems like this is a love reading but you also don't have too much subjective narrative cluttering your ability to cut to the heart of the matter.

How do I start pulling cards?

After speaking to your client and solidifying the intention, shuffle the cards however you like. I tend to start shuffling the moment I sit down with them, during the chit-chat, and keep going until we're ready to start the reading. Depending on how the conversation goes, this is the point where I decide what spread I will use for their reading. I give them the deck to cut. However, they like, and however many times they like, and then put it back together. I am not particular about this. Some readers have their clients cut the deck three times in a certain direction with their left hand. Sure, why not? Regardless, the deck will not be put back together wrong. When they hand it back to you, take a breath, focus your intention, say a prayer, and pull the damn things.

How will I know when to pull more cards?

Any time you feel like you're about to say uhh or feel a desire to dig deeper into a card's meaning,

Pull another card. Any time it seems like there is something more to a story, pull another card. If something doesn't feel right, pull another card. Don't be precious about this.

How will I know when I am done with the reading?

In a perfect world, every reading ends the same way as good sex—decisively, intuitively, and with both parties feeling satisfied. While my readings have a run time of one hour, I never set a timer for them. Maybe it's magic, maybe it's practice, maybe i've given enough readings to get into a groove of arcing a reading around the length of an hour, but they just seem to end right at the hour mark naturally. For me, a reading ending feels like a door closing, a definitive feeling that all information available to that person to aid them in their intention has been delivered. I leave a small window of time, in the end, to ask them if they have any questions, but this is to follow up on what's already been covered. In less than ideal scenarios, clients will push for more time or open up a completely new topic at the end of a reading. If it can be answered in a couple of cards, I will let it happen. But, if at the fifty-seven-minute mark someone says but what about my family? I let them know this is a subject too complicated to be appropriately assessed in the remaining time. It's not the best feeling in the world, but the client doesn't always have to be happy in order for a reading to be complete. I've painted comprehensive, practical pictures for clients of how to move forward from where they are, and sometimes where they are is such a shitshow that it doesn't look a whole lot better than where they are at the current time. This is okay. You are not a performing monkey. You are not reading tarot to tell people what they want to hear. If you feel like you do not have more information for them, that is how you know the reading is over.

I know you mention that it's hard to be wrong if you are aligned with your intuition, but real talk, what do you do when the person you're reading for says you're wrong?

Alright, my sweet, scared, doe-eyed little peaches. The honest-to-god truth is I don't really know how to answer this question. I waited for this nightmarish moment for years before accepting it probably wouldn't happen. Granted, I don't go into the depth that some mediums and intuitive do. I'm not going to try to pull your grandmother's name out of thin air or intuit the city your father is from. If this type of energy reading is something you are interested in, this book is not a resource for that and here's why: When giving a reading, I channel information from the highest available energetic source, which actually is not the person I'm reading for. It's their higher self; the spirit-clique, angel squad that reflects a truth greater and truer than a person's immediate perception of it. Specific information and details come in at a denser vibration as they are, really, of no consequence to the message and heart of the matter. However, they can be important if someone is coming in skeptical. Mediums—people who channel the departed—pull information from this more human, slightly heavier energetic layer to offer their clients proof of the living mind, of the person coming through. It can be as specific as a name or a relationship or as vague as a smell, but it will always be something that allows the client to recognize the person trying to communicate with them. I don't like doing mediumship. I find it viscerally invasive and emotionally draining. I will allow it in if it comes through during a reading, but I do not ask for it. I'm saying all this because these are the cold, hard facts that you can be objectively wrong about. I would advise not trying to provide information like this unless it specifically presents itself to your through your intuition. If you're wrong, that's okay. Ask a clarifying question and move on.

What I have experienced is abrasive, obnoxious clients who come in not wanting to hear the truth. One of them came into my apartment with a dog she didn't ask to bring with her, refused to moments of meeting them because she said she was unable to plug into that person's energetic field intuitively.

The best advice I can give you on being wrong in a reading does not differ much from being wrong in life—when you are, correct it and move on. When you're not, trust your integrity, hold your ground, and do not let yourself be bulldozed by assholes.

Chapter Fourteen
Tarot Myths Busted

No one really knows where the Tarot originated, but lots of theories abound.

- It's an ancient Egyptian system of divination
- The Atlanteans were told about it by aliens
- It was part of traditional Kabbalah
- It was invented by Romany Gypsies
- It's part of a complex magical system designed to achieve spiritual enlightenment
- [Insert your own myth here]

The reality is that, although the origins of Tarot are shrouded in mystery, we do know a certain amount about it and it's surprisingly mundane.

The Tarot first appeared sometime between 1420-40 in Northern Italy. Any visitor to Italy will be struck by how much Renaissance Italians loved, including symbolism in everything they do, and this new set of cards was no different. The precursor to our modern-day playing cards, Tarot, or Tarocchi as it was known back then, was originally used for card games, the divinatory aspect added in later, around the late 18th century.

That's it! No scary witchcraft or mysticism involved. It isn't related to any specific religion or tradition, so you can adapt it to your own personal spiritual practices or keep it as a tool, nothing more, nothing less. It works regardless of whether you have religious or spiritual beliefs or are totally atheist.

Despite this, several myths have grown up around Tarot and then insinuated themselves into our contemporary subconscious to the point that these myths alone are enough to put some people off going anywhere near a Tarot deck, which is a pity. It's one thing to decide you don't want to know about your future; it's quite another to decide you don't want to learn about Tarot because of some groundless superstition.

So, here are some of the most common Tarot myths and the reality behind them:

A Tarot is a tool of the devil/inherently evil

As we've already seen, Tarot cards evolved out of a simple game. Nothing evil there.

Tarot cards are printed pieces of card manufactured in a factory (unless you're lucky enough to have a very talented artist friend who can make some for you). Now, we can argue about the evils of industry, but that doesn't make the cards themselves a good or bad thing. They just are.

Any evil you may find in them comes from the reader's intention, not the cards.

You must never buy your own Tarot cards

Utter nonsense! I'm not sure why it would matter who bought your cards, but although my mother bought my first deck for me, I purchased the Rider-Waite deck I still use today, and it's always served me well.

While it's nice to have someone buy you a gift, choosing your own cards has the added advantage that you can select the deck that speaks to you. However you came about your cards, it won't make any difference to the accuracy of your readings.

You must never let anyone else use or touch your cards

If this one was true, it would be difficult for anyone to have a reading. I always get my clients to shuffle the cards if I'm doing an in-person reading since I feel it gives better results.

Sure, it's good to show respect for your tools, so you might not want to let a toddler with jam-streaked fingers rifle through your cards, but the reality is it doesn't matter how many people handle your cards. They'll still work.

You must store your Tarot cards in silk

No, you don't. You can store them however you like. Keeping them wrapped up in something beautiful creates a good impression for your clients, but it doesn't impact on the accuracy of your readings.

You must be psychic to read Tarot cards

While working with the Tarot can help you develop your psychic abilities, you don't need any innate abilities to interpret the cards. You're working with archetypal symbols that speak to our deepest subconscious. Your talent as a Tarot reader comes down to your connection with the images rather than any additional psychism. The cards will tell you everything you need to know. Stick with what you see in the symbols, and you won't go far wrong.

Tarot readings are 100% accurate

Aside from the fact that it's illegal to make claims of accuracy without proof, Tarot readers sometimes get things wrong. Even the best readers make mistakes.

A Tarot reading is a little like looking down the road you're currently traveling if you like your current destination, great! Keep going! If not, change what you're doing to go somewhere else. The whole point of a Tarot reading is to get advice on the best way forward, which might mean changing what you're doing. Once you've switched your course, you've automatically invalidated your reading, which means its predictions may not come true now.

Tarot readings must always be carried out in person

While I personally prefer to do a reading for my clients in person, it really isn't necessary. You can do phone readings and internet readings, and they'll still be just as accurate. The only difference is that you'll have to shuffle the cards on behalf of your client. That's it.

The Death card is a bad omen

It's natural to feel afraid when you get the Death card, but there are far more ominous cards in the deck. The Death card is more about change; the ending of one situation as a new one begins. Death is a natural part of the life cycle, clearing the way for something positive to develop.

While it's true that you could potentially read someone's death in the cards, it's highly unlikely, and even if it did come up, the Death card wouldn't tell you about it.

So, there you have it! A basic history of the Tarot alongside a few myths that should have been consigned to the history books a long time ago.

Chapter Fifteen

Summary...

In this chapter, you'll learn some more techniques on how to prepare yourself and also your cards before making a reading. It's very important that you are prepared not just mentally but also intuitively. All the tips, methods and techniques given in this book will only serve as your literal guide in interpreting the tarot cards but your intuition will ultimately become your "inner guide" to help you learn the true message of the cards that will help improve your clients' lives.

Using Narratives or Storytelling in Tarot Reading

Storytelling using tarot cards could be used as a tool for your imagination to tell a story that can enhance your reading skills and make you more familiar with the energies of your card. It's not about interpreting the literal meaning of the cards, it's more about using the images and symbols of the card and how a story may evolve or unfold once it is drawn. You can pull out three cards to represent the beginning of the story, another three for the middle of the story and three more cards for the conclusion of the story. You can use narratives in tarot reading to practice self – awareness and also be more familiar with your deck; it will also help you as a reader to allow the imagery of the cards to 'talk' to you. It's not about interpretation or discernment; it focuses more on your creative imagination process.

Take the time to work with the cards you draw and then try to determine what kind of story emerges from those cards. Reflect on it and also try to notice if the story is something that is similarly related to what's going on in your life.

As an example, you must set the scene, set the tone, and probably make up some characters for your first three cards since this will serve as the introduction of your story. Then the next set of three cards will serve as the climax of your story – so there's a dilemma or some kind of action to the story. Once you have move through the introduction and the climax, you can begin to formulate a narrative out of it and just let your mind flow without thinking about the meanings of each card, just focus on the image and draw a story from there. The last set of three cards will play out as the final outcome or ending of your narrative.

Narratives or practicing storytelling with your cards tells you as a reader that there's more to tarot card reading, it's not just about answering a query or about getting direct answers or guidance from it. It's a technique to help you broaden your imagination, use your creativity and basically learn more about yourself because that will help you become a much better and effective tarot reader.

Shuffling Your Cards

"To shuffle or not to shuffle?" This is the question most asked by beginners, and it's actually interesting because this is a 'big deal' when it comes to tarot reading since shuffling of cards is a process that happens before a reading, that's why many people are asking if there's actually a significance or if there's an impact to the reading if the cards are shuffled or not. It's sort of a way to prepare your cards for a tarot reading.

There's a lot of ways in which a tarot reader can do a reading and the shuffling or not shuffling of cards depends on what kind of reading is going to be implemented, the kinds of questions that will be asked by the client or the kind of method that will be used by the reader. The notion of how a reader should shuffle a card is related to the kind of layout or spread that you're going to use for a particular reading.

Some experts will tell you to sort of 'cleanse the card' by surrounding it with crystals or some kind of energy stones to clear out the energies from its previous reading so the cards can start anew, this is not required but it depends on you if you believe in that kind of philosophy. Another method you can use if you're doing a relatively simple questioning session or simple methods of layout is to just randomly 'shuffle' the cards on the table, make a pile while these cards are faced down and then let your client draw the card because it makes the subject responsible for the card they get.

Now if you're going to do a Celtic – Cross layout for the cards wherein you have to layout 10 cards and the positions as well as the connections of the cards matter, you can organize your deck by arranging the major arcana cards (0 – 21), followed by the minor cards (ace cards to King) with wands coming first, followed by cups, swords and last is pentacles. This kind of arrangement is only a suggestion; of course you can arrange your deck in which you see fit but that order is based on how the energies come down in the tree of life. Again, it's totally up to you, if you feel that the deck must be arrange in this way or that way for a particular reading or whatnot then it's your call. What's important is you arrange them in a certain way and not just randomly shuffle them since the Celtic – Cross layout is quite a complicated method of reading tarot.

For some readers, they let their clients shuffle and cut the cards in the most comfortable way possible, not like how dealers shuffle cards in the casino sort of thing (although it can be done too) but in a way where they will feel the cards in an intuitive level before stacking them up. Again, there is no exact method of shuffling or preparing your cards; these are merely guidelines of how to do it based from various tarot readers' experiences, at the end of the day it's up to you in finding your own style of doing things.

CONCLUSION

Now it is time to close the topic with a final summary and overview of tarot cards. Hopefully, this book will be a valuable resource for people who would like to have the tarot explained. It covers the known history of the tarot, possible speculation about ancient origins, and the meaning and interpretation of the actual card in the deck.

While the first actual surviving documentation of tarot card use only comes from Europe in about the 1400s, the symbols on the cards are much older. It is believed that the deck of cards traveled into Italy from countries in the Middle or Near East. Some people associate these symbols from the mystical Kabbalah or even the beliefs and practices of ancient Egyptian religions.

However, most scholars are not satisfied that there is any proof that the tarot came from an older society by itself. It is just as likely that later writers, in the late 19th to the early 20th century, assigned meanings from their own knowledge of ancient history to these cards.

However, an important thing to remember is the concept of synchronicity. This was actually developed by a famous psychologist named Carl Jung. It explains how events can happen that are very related in meaning without a causal relationship that is clear to human senses.

This is associated with the expression: There are no coincidences. This is how tarot scholars explain their art.

Shuffling the deck, placing cards in a particular spread, and then selecting interpretations may not be random but influenced by the law of synchronicity.

Human brains are very good at picking up on the meanings of symbols. They may even be better at this than always understanding the meanings or words. It is surely true that these symbols mean the same things to people all over the world, and that is not something that can be said of individual words.

In that way, the Tarot speaks to the reader and the questioner in a way that is relevant but still open to interpretation. The tarot deck, with all of its cards, is only a tool. A hammer or saw does not build a house. Likewise, a reader uses the deck as a tool for divination. In most cases, the quality of the reading depends upon the talent and intuition of the reader and not the deck of cards.

No card is either good or bad. They symbolize qualities, interactions, or events that may influence the questioner. In some cases, the cards could represent the questioner, but they may also draw attention to other people in the questioner's life.

For example, the Fool does not represent stupidity. It represents a carefree life. In some cases, a person who does not worry about the wrong things has good qualities. On the other hand, it could also represent some lack or responsibility or attention to detail that could be harmful. Each card must be taken in its context to be properly interpreted.

Also, tarot is considered a divination art. However, it is a mistake to believe that tarot is only there to predict the future. In fact, even parts of a spread that represent the future only represent a possible future if the present course of action isn't changed. That is why tarot is valuable. It helps the questioner understand what happened in the past, what is happening now, and how these events, relationships, or even attitudes may turn out in the future.

In the end, tarot often brings to light things that the questioner already knew. He or she just could not uncover the answers because of self-deception or because they were buried deep in the unconscious. For most people, using the tarot correctly does require learning about the tarot. However, mostly, it requires learning more about the questioner.

There is also not one best kind of tarot deck. Some are more popular than others. Frankly, some new tarot decks are even sort of silly. However, the cards are only cards. If they have the right symbols, and the reader can interpret those symbols, they work. Even online tarot decks can work. The most important thing is for a potential reader to find the tarot deck that appeals to them and then practices their art.

This brings the book to the topic of practice. Good readers do spend time studying symbols and meanings of tarot cards and tarot card patterns. However, the only way they really become good is by practicing. Great chefs probably own a lot of cookbooks, but they become great chefs by cooking. The same can be said about almost anything, and it is certainly true of tarot.

Now go out and practice. Find the right deck, learn to store and protect it, and begin practicing by performing readers on anybody with a question. It is entirely acceptable to begin by doing readings on the reader. However, some readers find that it is actually easier to perform readings on other people. Everybody knows people with questions. With proper study, honesty, and a willingness to have an open mind, it is possible to use the tarot to provide the right answers!

THANKS FOR READING!

The Complete Tarot: Learn The Tarot For Beginners & Advanced

I know you could have picked any number of books to read, but you picked this book and for that I am extremely grateful.

I hope that it added at value and quality to your everyday life. If so, it would be really nice if you could share this book with your friends and family by posting to [Facebook](#) and [Twitter](#).

If you enjoyed this book and found some benefit in reading this, I'd like to hear from you and hope that you could take some time to post a review. Your feedback and support will help this author to greatly improve his writing craft for future projects and make this book even better.

I want you, the reader, to know that your review is very important and so, if you'd like to leave a review, all you have to do is click here and away you go. I wish you all the best in your future success!

Thank you and good luck!

Sofia Visconti

A SPIRITUAL START!

Start your week with gratitude, joy, inspiration, and love.

Healing, motivation, inspiration, challenge and guidance straight to your inbox every week!

FIND OUT MORE

www.ingramcontent.com/pod-product-compliance
Lightning Source LLC
Chambersburg PA
CBHW071215080526
44587CB00013BA/1379